ORDINARY
IRISH LIFE

First published in 2013 by Irish Academic Press

8 Chapel Lane,
Sallins,
Co. Kildare,
Ireland

This edition © 2013 Irish Academic Press
Individual chapters © contributors

www.iap.ie

British Library Cataloguing in Publication Data
An entry can be found on request

ISBN 978 0 7165 3154 8 (cloth)
ISBN 978 0 7165 3177 7 (paper)
ISBN 978 0 7165 3210 1 (Ebook)

Library of Congress Cataloging-in-Publication Data
An entry can be found on request

Printed in Ireland by Sprint-print Ltd.

ORDINARY
IRISH LIFE

Music, Sport and Culture

EDITORS **Méabh Ní Fhuartháin** and **David M. Doyle**

IRISH ACADEMIC PRESS

This publication was grant-aided by the Publications Fund of the National University of Ireland,Galway/Rinneadh maoiniú ar an bhfoilseachán seo trí Chiste Foilseachán Ollscoil na hÉireann, Gaillimh.

Ionad an Léinn Éireannaigh
Centre for Irish Studies

CONTENTS

LIST OF
CONTRIBUTORS

GUY BEINER is a senior lecturer in modern European history at Ben-Gurion University of the Negev. He has a PhD in modern Irish history from University College Dublin and has been awarded research fellowships at Trinity College Dublin, the University of Notre Dame, the Central European University and the University of Oxford. His book, *Remembering the Year of the French: Irish Folk History and Social Memory* (University of Wisconsin Press), won numerous awards.

MARGARET BREHONY completed a PhD in 2012 entitled, *Irish Migration to Cuba 1835-45: Empire, Ethnicity, Slavery and 'Free' Labour.* Based at the Centre for Irish Studies, National University of Ireland, Galway, her doctoral research was funded through an Irish Research Council of the Humanities and Social Sciences (IRCHSS) scholarship. Previously, Margaret worked for five years with the Irish Refugee Council. She is also a member of the executive committee of the Society for Irish Latin American Studies (SILAS) and currently teaches part-time in Latin American Studies at NUI, Galway.

VERENA COMMINS is a doctoral student at the Centre for Irish Studies, NUI, Galway. Verena's PhD research concerns an appraisal of the Willie Clancy Summer School and its contexts for the performance, transmission and commemoration of Irish traditional music. A second generation Irish musician, her research interests include diasporic music-making experiences and practice. She is co-founder of Comhrá Ceoil, an Irish music and dance studies research group at NUI, Galway, where she currently lectures.

DAVID M. DOYLE is an Irish Research Council (IRC) Postdoctoral Fellow at the Institute of Criminology, University College Dublin, and a Research Associate of the School of Social Work and Social Policy, Trinity College, Dublin. A previous recipient of an IRCHSS doctoral scholarship, David has recently been awarded IRC New Ideas (2011) and New Foundations (2012) Awards to further his research on capital punishment in Ireland. His most recent publication (with Ian O'Donnell) is 'The Death Penalty in Post-Independence Ireland', *Journal of Legal History*, 33(1): 65–91.

FINOLA DOYLE-O'NEILL lectures on Irish Media and Film History at the School of History, UCC. She has previously worked as a journalist and radio/television presenter and co-authored *Media Skills for Teenagers* (2004). Her book, *Hosting a Nation*, charts the impact of Gay Byrne's *Late Late Show* and his radio show on Irish life (forthcoming, Cork University Press, 2013). She recently convened a conference, examining 50 years of television in Ireland, in conjunction with RTÉ.

LEO KEOHANE teaches at the Centre for Irish Studies, NUI, Galway. His primary areas of interest and research are counter-hegemonic theory and cultural studies. He is currently completing a biography of Captain Jack White DSO, founder of the Irish Citizen Army and one of Ireland's few self-professed anarchists of any significance.

REBECCA S. MILLER is Associate Professor of Music at Hampshire College, Amherst, Massachusetts. She received an MA from Wesleyan University and a PhD in ethnomusicology from Brown University. Miller is the author of *Carriacou String Band Serenade: Performing Identity in the Eastern Caribbean* (Wesleyan University Press, 2008). From 1982–1992, Miller was director of the Irish Arts Center's annual Irish traditional music festival in Snug Harbor, Staten Island, NY. Miller has conducted fieldwork as a Whiting Fellow in Ireland and is finishing a book on popular Irish music from the 1930s to 1975.

MÉABH NÍ FHUARTHÁIN is currently University Fellow (Teaching and Research) in Irish Studies at the Centre for Irish Studies, NUI, Galway. Méabh has published widely on Irish music and is popular music subject editor of the landmark *Encyclopedia of Music in Ireland* (forthcoming, UCD Press, 2013). A former IRCHSS recipient, she is consultant editor of Barry Taylor's forthcoming *Music in a Breeze of Wind: Traditional Dance Music of West Clare 1870-1970* (Clare, 2013).

LIAM O'CALLAGHAN is a lecturer at Liverpool Hope University, United Kingdom. Having obtained Bachelors and Masters degrees in history from University College Cork, he later completed his PhD at Leeds Metropolitan University. His first book *Rugby in Munster: A Social and Cultural History* (Cork University Press, 2011) was critically acclaimed. Liam has also been an invited conference speaker in the USA, Germany and Ireland and his work has been the basis of media interviews on RTÉ Radio, the *Irish Times* and the *Wall Street Journal*.

VIC RIGBY is a recently retired Fleet Street sports journalist. He developed a keen interest in Irish life and culture while taking a BA degree in history and politics as a mature student at Kingston University, London. He followed his undergraduate studies with an MA by research into the politics and culture of Irish rugby, focusing on the match between Ireland and Scotland in Belfast.

JIM SHANAHAN was educated at the University of Oxford and Trinity College Dublin. Jim currently lectures in the English Department of St Patrick's College, Drumcondra, Dublin and has published widely on eighteenth and nineteenth-century Irish fiction. A former IRCHSS Postdoctoral Fellow in TCD, he also worked as an editorial assistant on the *Dictionary of Irish Biography*.

LAUREN WEINTRAUB STOEBEL is a PhD candidate in ethnomusicology at City University of New York. She lived in Dublin from 2008–2010 while researching her dissertation on Comhaltas Ceoltóirí Éireann and the politics of musical community. Lauren has played Irish flute throughout New York City and Ireland, lectured in music at City University of New York and the Royal Irish Academy of Music, and worked with arts organisations such as Symphony Space in New York and the Smithsonian Folklife Festival, Washington.

ACKNOWLEDGEMENTS

We wish to thank all the participants at the second Galway Conference of Irish Studies, 2009 and the students and staff at the Centre for Irish Studies, NUI, Galway. Particular thanks go to Samantha Williams, Nessa Cronin and Louis de Paor for their support. We would also like to thank Lisa Hyde and Irish Academic Press for their encouragement, advice and expertise in bringing this collection to fruition. The support of the Centre for Irish Studies and the Grant in Aid of Publication Fund at NUI, Galway are also gratefully acknowledged. Thanks are also due to the peer reviewers and, finally, to the writers for their considered contributions.

1 PREFACE

MÉABH NÍ FHUARTHÁIN AND DAVID M. DOYLE

Collections of essays often reflect particular critical concerns at a given moment in time. This collection is no exception in this respect and has its roots in the interdisciplinary space created and encouraged at the Centre for Irish Studies, NUI Galway which challenges its students and researchers to engage not only with areas historically at the core of Irish Studies, but also other areas which have previously resided towards or even on the margins. The idea for a collection of essays pivoting around the theme of 'Ordinary Irish Life' was first mooted following the stimulating and successful second Galway Conference of Irish Studies (GCIS) in 2009, of which the editors of this collection were the principal organisers. The theme of that conference, 'Into the heartland of the ordinary', (from Seamus Heaney's *The Journey Back)* was deliberately chosen to suggest a peeling away, a back to basics approach and an invitation to explore the depth of meaning contained in the ordinary and everyday. We encouraged contributors to that conference to reveal sites of inquiry relating to the Irish quotidian experience. In doing so, the culture of ordinary life, sometimes overlooked or occluded in academic discourse, is engaged with in a meaningful way.

Building on the proceedings of the first Galway Conference of Irish Studies in 2006,[1] contributors were invited to submit essays pertinent to the theme and additional essays were sought from authors with a specific interest in the culture of ordinary Irish life. Among the many and varied papers presented at the conference several sub-themes emerged of where ordinary life might be fruitfully mined. The concentration of research in these areas was not sought exclusively — music, sport and culture are also sites in which the dynamic negotiation of ordinary Irish life is frequently played out. *Ordinary Irish Life: Music, Sport and Culture* thus seeks to excavate these sometimes neglected aspects of Irish life. In particular, these essays consider the relationship between 'ordinary' life and how meaning is constructed, negotiated and projected within the spheres of music, sport and culture, but also the processes through which the domain of the ordinary is reflective of the Irish experience and what it means to be Irish.

The meaning of ordinary Irish life is acutely explored in this collection through essays from both established and emerging scholars, in what we hope will be an important contribution to the interdisciplinary field of Irish Studies. The axis of Irish Studies, which developed during the twentieth century, is largely a literary-historical one, but there has been a shift away from this one-dimensional approach in recent years. It is noteworthy, for instance, that the cognate rather than sub-field of Irish Music Studies, vibrantly represented in this collection, is now an established research area, standing alongside its literary and historical brethren. Of course, academic debate does not exist in a vacuum and recent related publications in the area of culture studies in Ireland have already expanded the field of Irish Studies exponentially. This collection does not strive to replicate the extant work, but rather to complement it by drawing together the strands of music, sport and culture under the thematic umbrella of 'Ordinary Irish Life'.[2]

This collection offers new insights into the process of being Irish and its quotidian manifestations. Guy Beiner discloses the working and reworking of cultural content and meaning in 'Recycling Irish popular culture' as illustrated through the song text 'The Night Larry was Stretched'. Beiner articulates the osmotic fault lines between folk and popular culture historically and throughout the twentieth century. His work suggests a malleability of cultural interpretation, where context, performance and reception variously inform the end product and its derived meaning. A historical lens is also utilised by Margaret Brehony in 'Neither white nor free: Irish railroad workers in the troubled colony of Cuba, 1835–1837'. Brehony investigates the circumstances of how Irish workers found themselves in Cuba and the particular impact of Irishness on their day-to-day lives. The culture of the ordinary, as they experienced it in Ireland, necessarily shapes their experience of life in Cuba and the ensuing cultural encounters there. The 'reformulation of ethnicity' that took place leads to dramatic results in their 'ordinary' lives. 'Corner Boys in small town Ireland, 1922–1970', by Leo Keohane, identifies a culturally familiar but heretofore unexplored aspect of Irish life. 'Corner boys', a nebulous term by any standards, has nonetheless persisted in Irish ordinary life and Keohane traces its usage and the demarcations that surrounded it during the decades following the formation of the new state. His essay 'is less concerned with what corner boys were', than 'what they represented in the eyes of the general public'. A further contribution from Finola Doyle O'Neill, 'Life on-air: Talk radio and popular culture in Ireland' contextualises the development of talk radio in Ireland internationally and historically, and draws attention to the particularities of the ordinary Irish mediated experience.

Diverse discussions of Irish music culture range from Rebecca Miller's '"We were so different!" Negotiating Gender on the Showband Stage', which discusses the role of gender in the showband popular music genre in Ireland, to Lauren Weintraub Stoebel's, which expands Turino's model of community building and networks of practice in 'Rethinking Rural/Urban: Traditional Music and Musical Community in 21st-Century Dublin'. Verena Commins explicates one of the most important sites of traditional music cultural production in her contribution on the Willie Clancy Summer School. All three of these essays engage with the cultural domain of music making, from the showband stage to the session, to the classroom. Though discussing disparate genres (both popular and traditional Irish music) and in different time periods, all three essays are concerned with how music, as it is embedded in the lives of the ordinary evinces meaning. Vic Rigby and Liam O'Callaghan's account of 'The Riddle of Ravenhill: The 1954 Irish Rugby International in Belfast' and Jim Shanahan's essay, 'Seán Burke, Lion of Lahinch: an IRA man at the Walker Cup', both deconstruct the complex relationship between sport and politics in Ireland, and the intrusion of political pasts into subsequent domains of cultural engagement. These contributors first presented drafts of these chapters at the Sports History Ireland Conference, which was hosted by the Centre for Irish Studies in February 2007 and they made for 'fascinating listening'.[3] It is anticipated that they will now receive the wider readership that their scholarship merits.

We believe that Irish Studies should be configured as a field of research which investigates the lived and representative Irish experience and that this collection offers an insight into particular domains of ordinary Irish life in which meaning is worked out, debated and reconsidered. Through these essays, we hope to make a contribution to the expansion of the field of Irish Studies scholarship with the tethering of music, sport and culture at the heart of the discipline, not at its fringes.

Méabh Ní Fhuartháin and David M. Doyle
December 2012

2 RECYCLING IRISH POPULAR CULTURE

GUY BEINER

Conceptualisation of popular culture has baffled historians.[1] Cultural demarcations are inherently variable, as rigid distinctions between popular and elite, and between traditional and modern, are undermined by acknowledgment of inevitable reflexive interactions and by the realisation that these classifications change over time. Studies have documented the decline since the nineteenth century of traditional Irish popular culture.[2] Nonetheless, expressions of folk tradition continued to thrive and were continuously renewed. Though pretending to represent 'the ordinary', vernacular Irish popular culture was documented as 'folklore', reified as extraordinary and reproduced in different contexts, which allowed its popularity to cross multifarious cultural spheres of activity. The recycling and constant reinvention of popular culture can be demonstrated through a historical case study of an extremely popular ballad.

'The Night before Larry was Stretched' [also found as 'De Night before Larry was Stretch'd'] is a well-known Irish song, which, as this essay will show, enjoyed continuous widespread appeal for over two centuries. Steeped in colloquial figures of speech and rich in (quite literal) gallows humour, it depicts the last hours of a condemned Dublin criminal. A boisterous night of drinking, courtesy of friends who 'sweated their duds till they riz it' (pawned their clothes for the money) and card-playing around a candle-lit coffin ('six glims round his trap-case') ends in a fistfight. The commotion is interrupted by the obligatory visit of a priest, who is greeted with contempt, 'Larry tipp'd him a Kilmainham look, and pitch'd his big wig to the divil', and a graphic description is given of the outdoors execution proceedings on the following day, ending with brief mention of the burial, 'at darkey we waked him in clover, and sent him to take a ground-sweat'. It is one of a number of contemporary songs on prison life written in similar style. Another song, 'Mrs. Coffey', relates the reaction of Larry's wife and two sequel songs follow the story after the execution: 'Larry Coffey' (also found as 'Larry's Stiff') describes attempts to resuscitate the corpse, and 'Larry's Ghost', in which the eponymous hero fulfils his promise to 'come in a sheet to sweet Molly'. A couple of songs refer to another executed criminal – 'Luke Caffrey's Kilmainham Minit' ('Kilmainham Minuet' being a reference to a hanging) and 'Luke Caffrey's Ghost', though these do not appear to have achieved quite the same lasting popularity.[3]

Part of the appeal of such songs derives from the impression that they seem to offer a rare sense of the subculture of criminal life in eighteenth-century Dublin. This assumption should be pursued with caution. Comparably, James Kelly's study of printed 'last speeches' from the first half of the eighteenth century and Niall Ó Ciosáin's references to biographical crime fiction in the second half of the century reveal that these popular genres were highly stylised and cater to the wider sensibilities of society at the time.[4] The colourful 'Newgate cant', a nineteenth-century Dublin slang which expressively contributes to the allure of these songs, was apparently more widely familiar, since its idioms are also found elsewhere in English literature of the period.[5] Conceding that it cannot be determined whether the surviving texts of the songs are transcriptions or imitations of 'genuine popular compositions', Sean Connolly underlined their interest for historians: 'the picture they present is a vivid one: a plebeian counter-culture, characterised by celebration of the deeds of underworld heroes, a defiant awareness of the gallows, and a vigorous rejection of authority'.[6]

As is often the case with folklore sources, the precise origins of the song cannot be discerned. The earliest references in print date to the late eighteenth century. In 1787, the song appeared set to music in *Walker's Hibernian Magazine, or, Compendium of Entertaining Knowledge*, an Irish monthly that described itself as 'containing the greatest variety of the most curious and useful subjects in every branch of polite literature'.[7] The following year it was published (without music) in a chapbook printed in Monaghan, where it was described as 'an Irish slang song'.[8] It was already described then as being 'all the ton' [fashionable] in Dublin.[9] In 1791, the obituary of the German-born Jewish dulcimer player Isaac Isaacs, who enjoyed the patronage of the Dublin madam Margaret Leeson, lists 'The Night before Larry was Stretched' in his repertoire.[10] Towards the end of the century, it appeared in print as a broadside ballad.[11] In London, it was labelled 'a favourite song in all the convivial societies in Ireland'[12] and its air was identified as 'To the Hundreds of Drury I write', a song dating back to the early decades of the eighteenth century.[13] When included in *Paddy Whack's Bottle Companion* (1791), a collection of Irish songs published in London, it joined the fashionable comic depictions of stage Irishmen, which were embellished and distorted to amuse English audiences.[14]

Its appearance in *The Festival of Anacreon* (1789), the songbook of the Anacreontic Society, a gentleman's music club, is particularly revealing in terms of cultural affiliation. Simon McVeigh's study of London concert life argues that distinctions between musical professionals and amateurs were sharpened towards the end of the eighteenth century. Specific venues were associated with a social hierarchy, as outlined in a newspaper article: 'The HANOVER-SQUARE [Professional Concert] - QUALITY. The TOTENHAM-STREET [Concert of Ancient Music] - GENTRY. The FREEMASONS'-HALL [Academy of Ancient Music] - PEOPLE. And the ANACREONTIC [Society] - FOLKS'.[15] Though the compound term 'folklore' in its modern sense would only be coined by the antiquarian William John Thoms a half century later,[16] there was already a prevalent notion of vernacular culture associated with 'folk' with which the Anacreontic Society was linked. Founded in 1766 as a small dining club, which met in a coffee house on Ludgate Hill to sing glees and play instrumental music, it grew into an immensely popular bourgeois society, which by the 1780s met in a great hall-room at the Crown and Anchor Tavern in the Strand. Its meetings typically commenced with a West End-style symphonic concert (frequently playing the music of Mozart), followed by an elegant supper, after which songs were performed by theatrical singers and members (including notable vocalists). By midnight, the festivities deteriorated to more crude singing, described by one of its members as 'Improper Songs, and other vicious compositions', which included the Irish ballad. Ladies were expected to leave after the concert, though failure to do so was a recurring cause for complaint.[17] The hybrid character of the Anacreontic Society, which brought together stage actors, orchestra musicians and amateur singers, and its wide variety of music bridged between aristocratic and third-estate culture.

An advertisement for *The Festival of the Anacreon* notes: 'This collection, like every other of the same description, exhibits some puerile compositions, for which the Editor has the poet's plea in the *Beggar's Opera*, "This we must do to comply with the taste of the town".[18] The legitimisation concurred through reference to Rich Gay's celebrated *Beggar's Opera*, a cultural innovation that was probably inspired by Jonathan Swift's suggestion of a 'Newgate pastoral, among the whores and thieves there',[19] is apt. The *Beggar's Opera* deliberately crossed genres by recasting Italian opera in a plebeian setting and adapting lyrics to broadsheet ballads and folk tunes. Its London premiere at Lincoln's Inn Fields in January 1728 met with sensational success (setting a long-standing record of sixty-two consecutive nights).[20] In March 1728, it was staged in Dublin, where the tremendous popularity of its first season at the Smock Alley[21] triggered a vogue for English comic operas that persisted through the rest of the eighteenth century.[22] This trend is in part the context which enabled 'The Night before Larry was Stretched' to enjoy broad popular appeal.

Evidence of the ballad's growing popularity can be found in the setting of other songs to its tune, its title considered sufficiently familiar as to not require musical score or reference to the original air.[23] It was even familiar across the Atlantic, where its tune was applied in 1798 to a song satirising a notorious incident of political squabbling in Washington, which involved an Irish-American congressman.[24] 'The Night before Larry was Stretched' became a recognisable example of Irish popular culture and, as such, could find its way into contemporary English fiction. An early literary reference crops up in Robert Bisset's anti-Jacobin novel *Douglas* (1800), in which an Irish criminal claims to have known a 'choice fellow' in Dublin named Larry O' Donnell 'on him the song was made about'.[25]

If in mainland Britain the song was considered an entertaining specimen of Irish idiosyncrasy and could appear alongside a patriotic song eulogising admirals,[26] back in Dublin it inadvertently got caught up in the radical politics of the era of revolution. In 1789 the oppositional *Dublin Evening Post* published a couple of satirical songs denouncing informers, which were set to the tune of the ballad, as part of the editor John Magee's campaign against the pro-government *Freeman's Journal* and its proprietor, the government agent Francis O'Higgins (the 'Sham Squire').[27] More effectively, in its efforts to exploit popular culture in order to affect mass politicisation and bring 'the Republic to the Village', the propaganda of the secret society of the United Irishmen composed revolutionary songs set to familiar tunes.[28] A 1798 edition of their songbook *Paddy's Resource* includes 'The Chapter of Kings', which was sung to the air of 'The Night before Larry was Stretched'.[29] This biting republican satire of English monarchs re-adapted a lighter humorous song by the poet and actor John Collins, which he popularised through his performances in the role of an Irish schoolmaster in his musical the

Brush.[30] An 1803 edition of *Paddy's Resource* included the song 'Jemmy O'Brien's Minuet', which celebrated the hanging for murder of a notorious government agent in the service of Major Sirr (Dublin's feared chief of police). This composition was explicitly modelled on 'The Night before Larry was Stretched' and set to its tune.[31] Notably performed at 'de Sheriff's ridotto' on no. 1 Green Street,[32] it apparently caught on rapidly, appearing in several versions,[33] including a broadside on 'De sorrowful lamentation of De Bowld Jemmy O'Brien'.[34]

In 1799, during the heated pamphlet debate over the passing of the Act of Union, the air of 'The Night before Larry was Stretched' was used for an anti-union broadside.[35] A few years later, the air was adopted for the Dublin street ballad 'King William's Birthday' (or 'The Night Before Billy's Birth-Day'), which celebrated the defacement in November 1805 of the statue of King William on College Green, an act of political vandalism that infuriated loyalists and Orangemen.[36] In spite of such politicised adaptations, the source song was clearly not one of the many Irish rebel ballads, and continued to be published in its original form.[37] In the nineteenth century, though the text did not change substantially, the context for its reception shifted.

Following the passing of the Act of Union in 1800, a flourish of literary production engaged in explaining Ireland. Elucidation was directed both to an English readership, interested in familiarising itself with the customs and habits of the territory it had legally annexed, as well as to audiences in Ireland, not least the Anglo-Irish ascendancy, which in coming to terms with its recently acquired British status required a better understanding of Ireland's majority Catholic population. This cultural project is evident in the fiction of the time, typified by the novels of Maria Edgeworth and Lady Morgan (Sydney Owenson), and in the poetry and music of Thomas Moore's *Irish Melodies* (published in ten volumes between 1808 and 1834), all of which introduced to European salon culture an appreciation of romanticised adaptations of Irish traditional culture.[38] Descriptions of Ireland tended to play on stereotypes and stress the peculiarity of local traditions, as is particularly noticeable in the boom of travel literature.[39] An account of Dublin in 1822, which presented the city to English readers as 'a miniature of London', referred to the dialect of 'the lower orders' as 'of a most curious character, and which gave additional zest to their farcical sayings and jests'. Its fanciful depiction of Irish urban life, in which gentlemen visit convicts and enjoy their 'coarse low humour', identifies 'The Night before Larry was Stretched' as 'one of the best slang songs ever made'.[40] In light of romantic idealisation of the vernacular, Irish popular culture became a subject of curiosity.

In the cultural context of Union, Irish songs aroused keen interest. They were classified as a separate category in the multi-volume *The Universal Songster; or, Museum of Mirth*, which would be repeatedly reissued in new editions due, as acknowledged in the introduction, to 'rapid and extensive sale'. This compendium of course included 'The Night before Larry was Stretched', which it attributed to a man named Curran.[41] A telling example of how Irish songs were regarded at the time can be found in the songbook *The Shamrock*, published in 1830 in Glasgow, Edinburgh and London, distributed by booksellers in Dublin, Cork and Belfast, and advertised as 'the most versatile and comprehensive collection of Irish Songs extant'. In a 'copious historical introduction', Mr Weekes of the Theatre Royal in Drury Lane argued 'that Ireland's 'National Melody' has 'an exquisite melancholy in its character – a melancholy so profound, that the finest feelings of the human heart must, indeed, have been grievously wrung, to produce such an inimitable pathos'. Despite their allure, sentimental Irish songs were condescendingly berated as 'deficient in poetical attraction'. At the same time, Irish comic songs were credited with possessing 'the genuine spirit of an Irish bull'– defined as a mixture of oddity, humour and wit. The London actor acknowledged that 'these songs have, for a long period, constituted the principal dish at most convivial meetings, and have been sung at our theatres with the strongest marks of approbation, and must always maintain their popularity'.[42] Considered primitive yet amusing, Irish popular culture was fetishised through such late-Georgian notions of Celtic 'noble savagery'.

Exotic references to Irish popular culture became a staple of English popular culture. One of the Irish folk traditions that aroused particular curiosity, and with which the song became inadvertently associated, was the 'merry wake'. Fantasy played a role in shaping outsiders' perceptions of this tradition, which at the time was actually in decline due to Church opposition.[43] Charles Mulloys Westmacott, who in today's terms would be labelled a 'yellow journalist', composed in 1826 a poetic depiction of 'The Wake; or Teddy O'Rafferty's Last Appearance: A Scene in the Holy Land', which was styled in mock Hiberno-English and masqueraded as an authentic Irish composition.[44] Fabrication came easily to Westmacott, who would extort funds to suppress the publication of pseudo-satirical gossip. Under his editorship, the Tory newspaper the *Age*, like its liberal equivalent the *Satirist*, would represent a lowbrow popular culture quite apart from that of reputable papers such as the *Times*, though one which nonetheless entertained a broad, and often respectable, readership.[45] His anecdotal miscellany *The English Spy* (published in 1826 under the pseudonym Bernard Blackmantle) includes a narrative rendition of his wake poem, illustrated by the noted caricaturist Robert Cruikshank, in which 'The Night before Larry was Stretched' turns up 'among the most favourite ditties of the night'. The boisterous wake in this overdramatic account appears to mimic the nocturnal revelries in the prison song, as if to confirm the observation that 'there is a volatile something in the Irish character' and demonstrate how 'we often find them gay amidst the most appalling wants, and humorous even in the sight of cold mortality'. In a moment of candour, before delving into his trademark 'playfully satirical' register, Westmacott insisted that knowledge of the Irish cannot be gained from the Anglo-Irish 'wealthy absentees' or from the 'the lowly race, who driven forth by starving penury, crowd our more prosperous shores'.[46] The guiding logic of such pseudo-ethnography, which unabashedly dismissed

Irish testimony, preferred to imaginatively construe Irish popular culture on the basis of visitors' impressions.

Irish writers recognised the piquant of fanciful commentary on popular culture. Posing as Father Prout, parish priest of Watergrasshill in County Cork (purportedly the son of Dean Swift and Stella), the humourist Francis Sylvester Mahony, reproduced 'The Night before Larry was Stretched' in a satirical article on 'The Songs of France', which was first published in *Fraser's Magazine* in 1834. The song was attributed to Rev. Robert Burrowes, Anglican Dean of St. Fin Barre's Cathedral in Cork, rendered in liberal translation into French, renamed 'The Death of Socrates' [La Mort de Socrate] and discussed alongside references to the philosophers of the French Enlightenment and to the romantic novelist Victor Hugo.[47] This remarkable concoction was subsequently included in the multiple editions of *The Reliques of Father Prout* (supposedly edited by Oliver Yorke), which added an illustration of Larry's last night by the noted artist Daniel Maclise.[48] Claiming that 'nothing half so characteristic of the genuine Irish recklessness of death was ever penned by any national Labruyere [La Bruyère] as that incomparable elegy', Prout elevated the song to 'a most sublime Pindaric composition'.[49] Such literary mischief was typical of Mahony, who translated works of Thomas Moore into classical languages and accused him of plagiarism.[50] His creativity was appreciated for its literary merit; the *Saturday Review* praised the 'infinite adroitness' of his French translation of 'The Night before Larry was Stretched'.[51] Inserting a folk song into a discourse on refined literary culture, Mahony's parody mocked enlightenment models of top-down diffusion, whereby influences of élite culture were expected to trickle into popular culture, as well as romantic models of bottom-up gentrification, by which folklore is endorsed and integrated in national canons, insightfully suggesting that cultural dissemination can be reflexive and far more complex. Nearly a century later, the writer Padraic Colum would also make a French literary reference upon discussing the song, writing 'Baudelaire, one must believe, would have hailed this poem as a real Flower of Evil—the Satanic laughter is in it'.

Seeking to document actual popular culture, the antiquarian and pioneering folklorist Thomas Crofton Croker collected oral traditions, customs and folk songs. Although he intended to publish 'in the least offensive manner, a specimen of an Irish slang song' and acknowledged that 'The Night before Larry was Stretched' is 'the most popular song of this class', he omitted it from his *Popular Songs of Ireland* (1839) – the first of a number of folk music collections which he compiled for the Percy Society – on the grounds that 'there is much that is objectionable in it'.[52] Croker, an Anglo-Irish Protestant from Cork who worked as an Admiralty clerk in London, has been criticised for his aloofness towards the subaltern 'peasant' culture that he studied.[53] Contemporaries questioned the extent to which his collection was truly representative of popular culture. A reviewer in the *Morning Chronicle*, who argued that it neglects 'the songs of the middle class and the peasantry – the true depositories of Irish lyrical poetry', specifically faulted Croker for omitting 'the celebrated ditty of The Night before Larry was stretched', even though it was considered 'beyond all comparison the most remarkable production that was ever composed in the language of *slang*'. In contrast, Croker was admonished for including a 'wild anathema' composed by 'a mad-cap scarecrow itinerant rhymer'.[54] A review in the *Dublin University Magazine*, which denounced the collection's absence of 'patriotic effusion' and claimed that Croker was ignorant of 'thousands and tens of thousands of popular songs illustrating the habits of the people, their feelings, and their affections', noted: 'we protest against a volume of popular songs of Ireland, in which "'The night before Larry was Stretched'" is omitted from motives of refinement. What was ever more popular in Ireland that [than] this song'.[55] Victorians were both repulsed by, and attracted to, the perceived vulgarity of Irish popular culture and these conflicting attitudes were often conditioned by political persuasion. Whereas nationalists regarded local culture as a source of pride, which should be displayed without embarrassment, unionists tended to accentuate its primitiveness.

'The Night before Larry was Stretched' is discussed as a relic of bygone times, with particular attention being paid to the quaintness of the custom of celebrating on a condemned man's coffin, in the anonymously published *Sketches of Ireland Sixty Years Ago*, a racy account of Dublin eighteenth-century life, which went through numerous editions and was reissued in 1979 under the more fitting title of *Rakes and Ruffians*.[56] The author, John Edward Walsh, was a distinguished judge, who was fascinated with the Dublin underworld at the time of his father, Rev. Robert Walsh (a popular travel writer who provided much of the information for the book). Walsh's sensationalised portrayal of 'the rough prominences which distinguished our national character' and its 'degrading peculiarities' aimed to demonstrate progress: 'the contrast between what we *are* and what we *were* – between our present state of social peace, advancing enterprise, and regular habits, and the brutal violence, barbarism, and recklessness, from which we have emerged'. However, this implicit paean to the Union attempted to conceal the deep crisis of the Union in the year when it was published – 1847, notoriously known as Black '47, being the height of the Great Famine (euphemistically referred to in the preface as 'the gloom which at present overspreads us').[57] Whether from a nationalist or unionist perspective, romanticising popular culture entailed self-censorship.

Removed from its alleged demotic origins in a criminal subculture, 'The Night before Larry was Stretched' was domesticated in more polite Victorian settings, where it became a popular party piece. At a breakfast with leading English writers, Thomas Moore was astonished and amused to discover that Thomas Babington Macaulay was acquainted with it and could repeat it 'glibly', together with other Irish slang ballads.[58] At her last birthday dinner, during Christmas 1858, Lady Morgan sang it before her friends 'in a style that was inimitable'.[59] It was a source of constant interest for scholars of folk song, who pondered over its authorship, compared variations, and added annotations to elucidate the dialect, which was no longer familiar. Some commentators relished the far-fetched claim that it was written by a clergyman, unwittingly falling into the trap set by the prankster Mahony. The Anglo-Irish poet and folklorist Alfred Percival Graves, a founding member of the Irish Folk Song Society, called attention to this deception and tried to set the record straight by asserting authoritatively that 'This famous song has been long cruelly attributed to Dean Burrowes of Cork; but I have indisputable evidence before me that the Dean had no hand at all in the writing of it'.[60] The song's authorship remained, however, an intriguing puzzle.

Other commentators picked up on the attribution to Curran in the *Universal Songster* and speculated, rather improbably, that it may have been written by the celebrated lawyer and politician John Philpot Curran (1750–1817), though it does not match his poetic style. The name of the contemporary lawyer and poet Edward Lysaght (1763–1810), nicknamed 'pleasant Ned Lysaght' and well known in Dublin as a wit and bon vivant, was also floated as a possibility, but it was admitted that this claim was 'without foundation'.[61] The fanciful association of authorship with the legal profession would persist with the author Frank O'Connor – who considered the song 'one of the best poems in thieves' cant ever written' – insisting 'that it was certainly written by some member of the bar'.[62]

Edward Walsh noted a tradition that claimed that the song was the prizewinning entry in a competition of a Waterford literary society; it was allegedly submitted by an owner of a local cloth shop named Maher, known locally as 'Hurlfoot Bill', who 'continued to the end of his short and eccentric career of life to claim the authorship with confidence, "no man forbidding him"'.[63] Although Walsh acknowledged that this anecdote 'must go for *tantum quantum valet*' it was soon after endorsed as a legitimate claim.[64] In the absence of substantial biographical details, Maher's character would be further embellished. Henry Halliday Sparling, who criticised the 'carelessness or ignorance' of previous editors and took pride in publishing an 'unmutilated' version of the ballad, which he 'obtained by the careful collation of very many old chap-books and ballad-sheets', suggested that Maher was himself a criminal, 'worthy of the type he so well describes'.[65] A gloss to an annotated version of the song in John Stephen Farmer's *Musa Pedestris* (1896), a historical collection of canting songs and slang rhymes, admits that 'neither the authorship nor the date of these inimitable verses are definitely known' but attributes it nonetheless to Maher, who is converted from a shopkeeper into a shoemaker.[66]

The antiquated opaqueness of the text and its uncertain origins only added to its mystique. While considered typical of Irish popular culture, it was recognised as an 'extraordinary piece of poetic ribaldry'.[67] For some, its literary virtues were proof that it was composed by an educated writer 'as a sort of archaic exercise and ebullition of immorality', while others concurred with the American folklorist Alfred Mason Williams that it was 'a genuine street ballad', which originated in the authentic experience of anonymous 'Irish gallows poets'.[68]

Over the long nineteenth century, 'The Night before Larry was Stretched' continued to reappear in popular print. It was reissued on broadsides[69] and was regularly included in popular Irish song anthologies, such as *The Songs of Ireland*, which was edited for the Nation's 'Library of Ireland' by the Young Ireland poet Michael Barry and went through multiple editions.[70] New songs were often set to its tune, some of them became well-known in their own right, such as a comical song about Saint Patrick ('St. Patrick of Ireland, my dear!') composed by the Cork writer William Maginn in 1820,[71] while others were more ephemeral, such as a humorous song from 1858 named 'The Cats' Eyes', which was sold for a penny at the Poet's Box, probably in Glasgow.[72] Through its ubiquitous appearances in popular print it became a familiar reference, which was frequently alluded to and functioned as a marker for Irish popular culture. William Makepeace Thackeray referred to it as 'the most jovial song that I know of in the Irish language', adding (in line with his thesis that Irish culture is inherently melancholy) that 'along with the joviality, you always carry the impression of the hanging the next morning'.[73] Indicative of Anglo-Irish literature's avid preoccupation with popular culture, the song is mentioned in stories and novels written by leading authors, including Lady Morgan,[74] Samuel Lover,[75] Charles James Lever[76] and William Carleton.[77] It appeared on stage in Dion Boucicault's popular melodrama *The Colleen Bawn* (first performed in 1860),[78] and later in John Millington Synge's play *The Tinker's Wedding*,[79] a drama initially performed in London in 1909 but considered 'too immoral for Dublin', where it first played in the Abbey theatre only in 1971.[80] James Joyce, who had a penchant for Irish folk songs,[81] weaved it into the Cyclops episode of *Ulysses*, which takes place in a Dublin pub where 'considerable amusement was caused by the favourite Dublin streetsingers L-n-h-n and M-ll-g-n who sang *The Night before Larry was stretched* in their usual mirth-provoking fashion'.[82] Oliver St. John Gogarty, on whom the character of Joyce's Buck Mulligan ['M-ll-g-n' in the quotation above] is founded, dedicated a chapter to the song in his eighteenth-century period novel *Mad Grandeur*.[83]

In 1912, the ballad was illustrated by Jack B. Yeats and published by the Cuala Press, under the management of Elizabeth Corbett ('Lollie') Yeats, as the February instalment of 'A Broadside', a monthly series issued from 1908 to 1915.[84] Whereas broadsides in the eighteenth and nineteenth century were generally affordable and widely available, this exquisite revival of the genre, with a limited print run of 300 copies and sold by annual subscription for twelve shillings, was primarily aimed at a connoisseur audience.[85] Traditional popular culture had become an exclusive cultural artefact. Some seventy years later, the Northern Irish artist Hector McDonnell would follow in the footsteps of the eminent illustrators Robert Cruikshank, Daniel Maclise and Jack B. Yeats, who had previously provided visual interpretations of the song. His illustrated book version, which won the Irish Book Design Award in 1985, was published in 500 numbered copies and quickly became a collector's item.[86] By the late-twentieth-century, boundaries between high and popular culture had become blurred beyond recognition.

In the mid-sixties, Colm Ó Lochlainn's songbook *More Irish Street Ballads* (1965) would feed into the folk revival and re-introduce the song to a new generation of musicians and audiences.[87] The Dublin balladeer Frank Harte recorded a version based on Ó Lochlainn's lyrics in 1967.[88] Popular celebrity singers, whose concerts filled large venues, picked up their songs from veteran local singers, who had previously performed in pubs and other such intimate settings. Christy Moore, for example, claimed to have learned 'The Night before Larry was Stretched' from Andy Rynne of Prosperous, County Kildare.[89] The song has since featured on albums of internationally successful bands, such as the Wolfe Tones.[90] When sung by the rock star Elvis Costello, it transcended the niche audience of traditional music and entered the realm of global popular music.[91] In an age of increasingly visual popular culture, it was even adapted to the big screen. The recovery and digital restoration in 1998 of the long-lost footage of the avant-garde film 'O'Donoghue's Opera' enabled its debut in Ireland, followed by its international release.[92] Filmed in 1965, the movie humorously dramatises 'The Night before Larry was Stretched' with the Dubliner's Ronnie Drew – an iconic figure of the folk revival – in the leading role. Mainly set in Baggot Street's O'Donoghue's pub – a popular Dublin venue with a reputation for live traditional music sessions, it opens with a rendition of the ballad by the folk singer Johnny Moynihan and includes appearances of other celebrated folk artists (Seamus Ennis, the Dubliners, the McKenna Folk Group and the Grehan Sisters). This bohemian cinematographic gem paraphrased the *Beggar's Opera* (through the filtering influence of the *Threepenny Opera*), locating Irish traditional popular culture once more at the cutting edge of cultural production.

Since its first appearance, 'The Night before Larry was Stretched' has provided immeasurable entertainment to a diverse range of audiences and readers and has appeared in many different spheres of popular culture. It was considered a representation of a local subculture and acclaimed as a showpiece of a national folk culture. Though distinctly Irish, its popularity transcended Ireland and, ever since its early appearance in London, it enjoyed success in Britain, ultimately entering a global mass culture of popular music. Sung as a street ballad in rough and ready circumstances and performed in genteel settings, its appeal crossed social strata and cultural milieus. Recycled endlessly in popular print, it was often mentioned in literary circles and repeatedly referenced in amateur scholarship. Its inclusion in the canon of Irish poetry, as defined by authoritative anthologies edited by academic experts, defies clear-cut distinctions between highbrow and lowbrow culture.[93] Whereas Irish folklore studies has typically focused on rural culture, it is an innately urban song. The concept of 'folk music' was constructed and repeatedly redefined throughout the period,[94] and the variety of references to the ballad seems to concur with Philip Bohlman's observation that 'folk music has often demonstrated a peculiar resistance to systematic classification', and might even suggest that this maxim could be applied to popular culture at large.[95]

Overall, the history of the ways in which the ballad was recycled over two centuries demonstrates that references to a folklore tradition can serve as an index of attitudes to Irish popular culture. In this regard, it is not so much the changes in the song over time, but rather how it was perceived and referred to, which are of particular interest. Contrary to prevailing critiques of folk song collecting, documentation and revival of the song did not result in fabrication of its text.[96] Though it was open to individual interpretations in performance and several variations have been documented, the ballad mostly remained a set text sang to the same tune. By and large, its transformations were contextual rather than textual, reflecting reformulation of perceptions of Irish tradition, which reveal how the concept of Irish popular culture was constantly reinvented and regenerated, allowing it to maintain its popularity.

3 'WE WERE SO DIFFERENT!': NEGOTIATING GENDER ON THE SHOWBAND STAGE

REBECCA S. MILLER

In 1962, Mildred Beirne of Co. Mayo went out on her first music job with the Granada Girls Showband, one of the rare – if not the only – all women showbands in Ireland.[1] She and four other young women, ranging in age from 16 to 18, drove with their band manager, Leo Beirne, to Killybegs, Co. Donegal. After a stop to buy sweets, they arrived at the dance hall and set up their equipment, had their tea, and then played until 3:00 am. Mildred Beirne sang and played the drums and then went out on the dance floor and danced the steps to the hit 'The Hucklebuck'.

Before the show, the Granada Girls received permission from their band manager to watch the fishing boats come into the docks in Killybegs. There, the fishermen gave each young woman a bag of fish to take home with them.

> Can you imagine the smell in the van coming home? … But, for me … I had a bag of fish … And when I landed home, Leo Beirne

gave me a pound note. Like, that to me was heaven. I had money and I had food. And you know … from that day to this, I was never short of either money or food.[2]

Mildred Beirne's account speaks to a number of economic and social conditions in Ireland in the late 1950s and early 1960s. She lived at home with her mother and, like many, was unemployed.[3] Unemployment was widespread among married women like Mildred Beirne's mother throughout the 1950s as a result of the lasting effects of the 1932 Marriage Ban. This law saw the compulsory retirement of female teachers upon marriage and, later, was extended to the entire civil service. The marriage ban was repealed among teachers in 1958, but according to Diarmaid Ferriter, there was 'still an ethos predicated on the idea that a woman working was acceptable in terms of economic necessity, but intolerable in the context of them having independent career ambitions'.[4] Mildred and her mother survived on money sent home by her father and siblings who, like thousands of Irish, had emigrated to London throughout the 1940s and 1950s to find work.

Playing in a showband, at that time an utter rarity for women, offered Mildred Beirne some degree of financial stability and the potential to provide for herself and her mother.

In the 50s and early 60s, there was no jobs. There really wasn't a job. You just simply left and took the boat and went to England and got a job there. There was very little education. I know, my older sister, she got educated … She was the only one of eight of us that were sent to school.[5]

Mildred's membership in the Granada Girls Showband also widened her world view and offered her a glimpse of the broader possibilities for a young person. Playing in a showband became for her and others like her, an antidote to Ireland's social poverty born of economic deprivation.

Indeed, former dance hall owner and later, Ireland's Taoiseach, Albert Reynolds, remembers this era for its pervasive sense of 'hopelessness' in the absence of opportunity and change.[6] Given the high rate of unemployment, particularly in rural Ireland, many young people had limited opportunities and impaired visions of their potential. In this way, Mildred Beirne was lucky that she found employment as a showband musician as it offered her opportunities beyond standard expectations.

Mildred Beirne's years in the Granada Girls Showband, though unusual, point also to the many social and economic changes afoot in Ireland at the time, including the growth of Ireland's nascent popular music industry as well as the changing role of women in Irish culture. Not only was Ireland's economic growth a factor in the rapid expansion of showbands, but the showband industry itself contributed to Ireland's economic recovery. The growth of showbands and Ireland's revitalised economy in turn offered unprecedented opportunities for a small but significant number of women. As they made headway into the showband scene, these women encountered opportunities to define who they were and how they wanted to be perceived on stage.

Showbands and Girl Singers

The musical phenomenon that launched Mildred Beirne and a handful of other women into successful musical careers was the showband – a specifically Irish musical response to the sounds and rhythms of American rock and roll and English pop songs. The first showband – the Clipper Carlton – originated in Strabane, Co. Tyrone, in the mid-1950s. This group of seven musicians put a 'show' into their performance, thus turning their audience's attention towards the stage. Within a short time, the showband phenomenon swept across Ireland with bands of all skill levels performing in dance halls and ballrooms throughout Ireland and Northern Ireland. These stage performances riveted Irish youth, dismayed parish priests, and ultimately revolutionised popular entertainment in Ireland. With an estimated 800 groups criss-crossing

Ireland in their vans to perform in cavernous dance halls up to six nights a week during the peak years between 1960 and 1975, the showband phenomenon quickly became an important industry.

Showband musicians aimed to keep their audiences entertained and dancing; to do so, they learned the newest hits from American and British radio broadcasts and brought these sounds as well as provocative choreographies to audiences that often numbered in the thousands. Typically consisting of electric guitar and bass, drums, piano, a charismatic lead singer and a brass section (typically trombone, trumpet, and saxophone), showbands performed an eclectic mix of covers of American rock 'n roll, country and western songs from the UK Top 10 and popular Irish songs. As interpreters of popular music, showband musicians learned hits from radio broadcasts from the US and England – on the BBC, the American Armed Forces Network and Radio Luxembourg. Showbands personified for their young audiences the otherwise faceless popular American rock 'n roll artists heard on the radio.

These bands introduced a radically new and different musical aesthetic from the sit-down dance orchestras that had – until that point – dominated dance halls and ballrooms. A typical 1930s or 1940s Irish dance orchestra ranged from six to sixteen players who sat while playing and read from arranged parts placed on music stands. With a few notable exceptions, dance orchestra members rarely looked up from their music to watch the audience. There was little improvisation and virtually no swing. In contrast, showband musicians jettisoned notated music and music stands, stood while playing and made eye contact with their dancing audiences. Moreover, they were now free to move or dance on stage. Through incorporating light choreographies and the occasional comedic skit into their performance, early showband artists put on a 'show', thus earning the genre its name.

While big band dance orchestras sometimes featured a 'girl singer', the role of women in these sit down dance orchestras was minimal: they alternated with a male vocalist in singing a song or a set of songs sandwiched in between sets of instrumental dance music. In contrast, women showband singers later often became the central attraction of the band, and in some instances, went on to lead their own groups. Overwhelmingly, however, the popular music scene in the 1950s and 1960s was a male dominated culture. With the exception of a handful of 'girl' singers and even fewer instrumentalists, the vast majority of showband musicians, managers, agents, dance hall owners, and record producers were men. Women showband artists were thus faced with successfully navigating the dual identities of being female and being a performing artist. Working in a man's world came with the challenges of touring; sexual harassment by bandmates and audience members; feelings of disempowerment in terms of decision making; of avoiding, or dealing with, financial exploitation; and the less visceral but important challenge of maintaining a sense of self on and off stage. To this end, women showband artists developed aesthetic and performance strategies. Some embraced the images of British pop icons or American country artists who heralded a sense of modernity and belonging to a larger world outside of Ireland. Almost all focused on cultivating expertise in one specific music genre, for example, pop ballads or country songs. And all of the women showband artists cultivated a stage persona designed to please their audiences while also positively reinforcing their status as women and as performers.

Setting the Stage: Transformation, Economic Change and Gender

The early 1960s saw the beginning of Ireland's transformation from an isolated and inward-looking culture to one that increasingly looked towards modern aesthetics from the US and the UK. Domestic and international economic development policies similarly moved the nation out from what had been a generation of economic isolation. Ireland's chronically floundering and under-developed economy and infrastructure were exacerbated by high unemployment rates that reached a record 78,000 in 1957[7] and by emigration numbers that, in the following year, totalled 60,000. Indeed, between 1951 and 1961, Ireland saw over 412,000 citizens emigrate, primarily to England and the United States.[8] Compounding this were anti-modernist and anti-intellectual mentalities derived from Ireland's neutrality during World War II – visions reinforced in Taoiseach Éamon de Valera's memorable 1949 radio broadcast that presented Ireland as a 'parochial, rural, neo-Gaelic, and above all, Catholic arcadia'.[9] In 1955, de Valera appointed T.K. Whitaker to the post of Secretary to the Department of Finance who brought with him a vision of Irish economic reform. Beginning in 1960, Ireland began to see its economy turn around and by 1967, the economy started to expand at a comparatively unheard of rate of four per cent per annum.[10]

G.J. Barker-Benfield has demonstrated that with national economic change come new definitions of male and female activity.[11] This was particularly true in the instance of Irish showbands. In contrast to the 'girl singers' in the previous era's sit down dance orchestras, the role of women in showbands shifted from often being under-used adornments to having a more central role on stage and in their band's overall hierarchy. But these developments were gradual and, like most processes involving the politics and social understandings of gender, cannot be viewed in absolute terms. Jazz scholar Sherrie Tucker writes that the stories that she collected regarding all-women jazz and swing bands 'were far too complex to fit neatly into the heroic pattern (she) had anticipated'.[12] Like Tucker, I heard stories told by female showband members that celebrated the showband era as a time of progress for women on stage; I also heard stories that bitterly recalled the ongoing marginalisation of woman as artist and the entrenched perception by audiences and bandmates alike of women performers as ornamental:

Sandy Kelly: The male singers in those bands always saw the woman (singers), for the most part … (as) a window dressing … The woman was expected to dress sexy. Wear a short skirt, or, at those times you were showing your belly and stuff like that … So you were expected to stand there, and wait your turn, and come and sing whenever it was your turn. And smile and look cute.[13]

Tina Tully: it was (a male world), it was. But, sure, I loved that. I did … Because they respected me, and that's one thing that's needed in a band like that.[14]

Further complicating the perception and treatment of women in the showband era was the fact that many grew into outstanding singers and in a minority of instances, proficient instrumentalists. The mastery of these types of performance skills, as Tucker suggests, presents the 'classic paradox of what it means to cross the gender division of labour'. Women knew that what they were doing was considered a 'man's job', an understanding amplified by the supposition by men (and some women alike) that 'women can't play'.[15] Yet, women showband artists demonstrated that they clearly could and did develop the requisite vocal and/or instrumental skills, further contesting entrenched assumptions.

Moreover, women showband artists found receptive audiences, particularly among young women whose experiences and desires matched their own. Caitríona Clear argues that the stage was set in the years just after World War II when Irish women were already starting to rethink what they wanted for themselves. By the early 1960s, Irish women were experiencing a changing set of expectations, including choosing to work rather than marry, thus heralding a 'coming of age of a generation of women who wanted to change their lives'.[16] At this time, too, emigration slowed as newly created jobs put money into the pockets of young Irish women, resulting in their presence in public spaces, such as dance halls. What these women encountered in these dance halls and ballrooms was typically an all-male showband, but occasionally, they would find one that featured a woman singer.

Among the best known female showband pop vocalists were Eileen Reid of the Cadets, Eleanor Toner with the Hilton Showband, Muriel Day of the Dave Glover Band, Penny Trent of the Millionaires, Amy Hayden of the Hoedowners, Eileen Kelly of the Nevada Showband and Tina Tully of the Mexicans. Many of these artists modelled their performance practice after such British pop artists as Petula Clark, Lulu (who toured with The Hollies in the 1960s) and British pop icons Dusty Springfield and Cilla Black. By the mid-1960s, the Motown style of song arrangement and the emergence of Motown girl groups proved inspirational to such women performers as the Irish pop trio, Maxi, Dick and Twink. Still others started out in the showband world but eventually turned to country and western music (which eventually became known as Country and Irish). Irish singers such as Maisie McDaniels, Sandy Kelly, Margo O'Donnell and Philomena Begley were inspired by Nashville icons such as Patsy Cline, Dolly Parton and Jean Shepherd.

Only a handful of women performed in showbands as instrumentalists, including electric bassist Patsy Fayne of the Exciters Showband (and later Paddywagon) and the members of the Mayo-based Granada Girls Showband (bassist/Hawaiian guitarist Anne Coleman; Stephanie O'Connor on mandolin and saxophone; accordion/cordovox player Mary Morris; saxophonist Kathleen Maxwell and Mildred Beirne on drums). Women vocalists sometimes accompanied themselves on acoustic guitar, notably Twink (Adele King) of the women's vocal trio, Maxi, Dick, and Twink.

Starting Out: 'Showband Looking for Girl Singer'

Like many of their male counterparts, the typical woman showband musician was a teenager, sometimes as young as 13 years old, at the time of joining a band. She often came into the showband world with a background as an amateur singer, perhaps as part of a choir or local singing group, and might have also been an avid dancer at dancehalls prior to joining the showband. Some women were literally born into the world of commercial music and performance. Showband singer Sandy Kelly, for example, first appeared on stage as an infant in her family's fit-up (travelling variety show), Dusky's Road Show.

> I was carried on stage as a baby. For the parts in plays. And then from once I could walk, I was doing everything from Shirley Temple to assisting the magician, to … [playing] child parts in the plays. And it was a magical childhood![17]

Other women found their way into showbands through responding to an advertisement placed in the local newspaper that specifically sought a female vocalist. These advertisements typically required a photograph and then an audition, as was the case with vocalist Muriel Day (née Galway), who, at the age of eighteen, answered an advertisement placed by the Belfast-based Dave Glover Showband.

> [Dave Glover] had an ad in the newspaper, looking for a girl singer. And I sent him a photo and a letter with my [singing] experience … But Dave didn't even answer my letter, because he didn't like my photograph.
>
> (At the time,) I was singing with a little [skiffle] band called The Saints … And in the meantime, Dave couldn't get a singer and he was … talking to this guy … [who] said 'There's a wee girl called Muriel Galway … and she's quite good'. And Dave said, 'I seem to know that name', but he said, 'where would I hear her?' So he came up to hear me … and someone said 'Dave Glover's here to see you'. And I said 'I don't want to see Mr. Glover. He was very rude to me, he didn't reply to my letter'. So I didn't want to talk to him. But eventually I auditioned for him … I sang my first song and then the rest of the band would do their thing and then he'd get me up again … I sang the same three songs all night because that's all I knew.[18]

After joining the band, Muriel Day was given instructions on how to comport herself on stage by Dave Glover.

> [Dave] taught me all sorts of stage presence because I didn't have any … He taught me to relax, first of all. And how to use the microphone at the correct distance, so that it wouldn't distort. How I could take it off the stand and walk around, if I wanted to, rather than be standing still. Just, presence.[19]

Bandleaders like Dave Glover not only helped mould some of the women singers, but they also handpicked them. Tina Tully entered and won a local talent contest in 1964 in England, where she was working at the time. Her accomplishment made the local papers back in her native Greystones, Co. Wicklow. Tommy Hayden, then the manager of The Mexicans, read of her success and sent her a telegram, asking her to join the band, which she did the following week.[20] Finally, other women singers came into the showband world by being in the right place at the right time. While still in school, the members of the 1970s pop vocal trio, Maxi, Dick and Twink, sang in a large choir; through this, they heard of an opportunity to audition as back-up singers for the newly-established Pye Records in Ireland. Maxi McCoubrey recalls:

> We would be backing the early, early showband records, and you never knew who they were, you just were told what to sing. So you'd come in and then they'd say, 'Sing this', 'Sing that', 'sing the other'. Sometimes they'd be there, the band guys, sometimes they wouldn't, you'd just [do] overdubs. So every song that you can hear in the late '60s to the '70s, we would've been on it … singing ooh-pa-pas and all of that.[21]

Eileen Kelly (known on stage as 'Kelley') moved into the showband world also having been a member of her school choir in Cork City and, following that, as a vocalist in the Music Makers, a semi-professional showband. In 1964, at the age of 19, she replaced the popular Maisie McDaniel in the Nevada Showband.[22] Kelley remembers eagerly moving into this very public world of full-time performance and travel; in doing so, she left behind the standard expectations of marriage and children that were typical for women in her generation. Complete independence was not immediately hers, however, as her professional career began only after an agreement was struck between her father, her then-fiancé, and showband impresario and manager of the Nevada Showband, George O'Reilly.

> George O'Reilly actually brought [my father] to Dublin and ... he told him that he was going to give me a three-year contract and what was involved money-wise. I was engaged to be married at the time ... And my boyfriend didn't want to know. He just didn't want to know. But the two of them, my father and him, both signed the contract ... they agreed with George ... I think George was afraid that my boyfriend might kick up, and that he might say, ... [George] showed [my father] what was involved and that I'd maybe put so much money away and all that for the marriage ... And my father agreed then.[23]

Kelley's experience underscores the expanded role of the showband manager who, like band leaders, often exerted a strong hand in selecting and moulding the image of the band and, in particular, the women singers. George O'Reilly spent considerable time developing Kelley's image as both a singer in the Nevada Showband and as a fashion pop icon. Encouraging her to look towards London fashions and women pop stars such as Petula Clark and Twiggy, O'Reilly constructed Kelley's image and then aggressively marketed it.

> There was also a dressmaker associated with George O'Reilly's office ... She made some stuff for me and ... it was very elegant, very nicely done, very beautifully cut ... Although (George)

generally left it to this woman … he'd say, 'Well, maybe if you wore something darker, that would kind of fit in with what the lads are wearing', and then if he saw something on you that he liked, he'd also admire it and say, something like, 'Hmm, that does become you'.[24]

George knew everybody! He was in touch with everything that went on in the business. And he could pick up a phone and ring anybody, the model agencies, you know … he had all the media onboard so I was always going to the hairdressers, going from the hairdressers to lunch with the press, going from lunch, maybe to dinner with the press. Going from dinner, then maybe, to have photographs taken with the band or without the band. I was always going, going, going.[25]

Playing to Survive: On the Road with Showband Women

In their heyday, semi-professional and professional showbands typically performed up to six nights a week throughout Ireland and Northern Ireland, often driving their mini-vans enormous distances on ill-paved roads to get from one show to the next. Upon arriving at the venue, they (or their roadies if they were a professional band) set up their sound system, then ate an early evening meal, changed into their stage costumes and started the show. A performance was likely to last five or six hours, with only one break, if that. At the end of the evening, members of the professional bands might then stay over in a hotel, but most semi-pro or amateur showband artists broke down the gear, packed it up and drove home.

Like their male counterparts, women showband artists remember the pleasure of singing — the sheer elation of performance — and the adulation of fans everywhere. But they also recall the exhaustion and tedium of near-constant travel, as well as physical challenges they experienced as women in a male-dominated world. A universal complaint was that few dance halls provided facilities for women artists;

performances at marquees that pre-dated the larger dance halls, were even worse:

> Margo O'Donnell: When I came onto the showband scene, it was totally a male orientated world. Like there was no dressing rooms for a girl, there was no facilities for a girl, it was just man, man, man, man. And they didn't really accept us, and you had to fight all the harder … if we were on in the marquee, we changed in the barn, we changed in fields. There was nothing there for the women.[26]
>
> Eileen Kelly: I'll give you an example of what happened to me when we arrived at a gig. It was lashing, lashing, lashing, pelting rain … So we arrived in with our mini-bus … But we got stuck halfway between the marquee and the gate. And now, in this lashings of rain, in a field that's all muck and mud, and for somebody like me, who's wearing white boots and maybe a miniskirt … the hair's all done, the makeup's all done, and you've got to get in there to get on that stage … So I was lifted. I was carried in and just plonked onto the stage. The place was packed with people, so we got the gig done and then we got back out and back on the road … Oh, yeah, you had to put up with the good and you had to put up with the bad.[27]

In addition to the vagaries of touring, there were less visceral but possibly more disturbing challenges of working as a woman in a man's world. Some women mentioned the denigration they experienced at the hands of the men they performed with and the sense that these men simply did not like their presence in the band. Eileen Reid, for example, recalls that there was strong opposition from members of the band when she was hired as lead singer in the Cadets: 'When the boys found out, they nearly had a fit.'[28] Margo O'Donnell remembers that she had to establish herself as a bona fide singer before being accepted.[29] Once in the showband world, women performers discovered that they were often not allowed to make decisions about performances or recordings, despite, as O'Donnell remarks, that she was 'the voice that would sell the product'.[30] In terms of band dynamics, some women found that their male counterparts did not necessarily welcome their musical ideas nor did they take kindly to musical instruction. Sandy Kelly, for example, found it easier to talk to her bandmates through her husband, who managed the band.[31]

The frequency of female showband artists marrying fellow band members was indicative of yet another issue common to women showband artists: due to their near constant touring away from home, the chances of meeting and marrying somebody outside of the showband world were slim. Eileen Reid recalled: 'You couldn't have a relationship with anyone. I mean … you'd never see them'.[32]

Finally, there was also the very real threat of physical assault. Most of the women I spoke with remembered the need to keep an eye out for inappropriate behaviour by male audience members and some indicated that they had been sexually harassed by band members. Still others remembered incidents of being mauled by fans rushing the stage and more than once, I heard about women performers literally being hauled off the stage by an audience member and carried to the back of the hall before being rescued by a bandmate.

There were also clearly many moments of satisfaction and happiness associated with performing in a showband. The prestige of being on stage often rivalled the sheer pleasure derived from performance.

Philomena Begley: I just loved getting on the stage and I just loved entertaining the people and, especially in concerts and cabaret and that. I would always get down on the floor and go around the audience, have a bit of craic and chat to them. Sit on their knee, do all the things and embarrass everybody … I was never one for sitting in the dressing room waiting for, you know, waiting for the big introduction.[33]

Maxi McCoubrey, now a radio presenter, remembers the constant social stimulation, the camaraderie of her bandmates and her delight in connecting with the audiences:

> It was a great meeting place for people and to this day, it's people I met there that remember you all the time. And part of my audience on radio are people who say 'I remember you in the Marquee in Drumlish' and I go 'Yeah, I remember it too'.[34]

Others point to the adulation of audiences and the opportunities that came with a life of performance.

> Muriel Day: I just loved it … if you were a popular show band, when you got on the stage there were maybe … 1,500, 2,000 people, and they were all standing close up to the stage, as close as they could get. All standing. And when you came on, you could have played for half an hour and nobody would have danced. They were just standing there applauding. That's magic.[35]

> Eileen Kelly: My life opened up unbelievably when I came into this business. I met so many people and I did so many things and I was at all these receptions and dinners and pubs. I was a playgirl … And a nocturnal animal … I was … out and about at all the parties and all the dos. I really lived![36]

While performing in a showband was surely exciting, most women performers embraced the stage, at least initially, because it offered a source of income, particularly in the early years when unemployment was very high in Ireland. And it was good money. Musicians, promoters, managers, agents, workers, dance hall owners alike remember the showband industry as enormously profitable. The wages that even an amateur or semi-professional musician could earn in a six-day week of performances often involved unheard of sums — earnings that allowed women to support their extended families and experience unprecedented levels of independence. For example, Mildred Beirne was delighted to earn a single £1 from her first job with the Granada Girls Showband in 1962; her pay increased over time and by 1965, as a full-time band member, she was earning nearly £50 per week.

> Now the most we would get would be maybe £6, £7 a night. That was a lot of money in '65, '66 and we were seven nights a week playing … All [my earnings] went to the house and to maybe buy clothes or shoes or something but … I was never hungry after that and I was never short of money.[37]

Women showband artists could earn substantially more performing than from the jobs typically available to them at the time. As the new lead singer with the Dave Glover Band, 19-year-old Muriel Day initially earned £20 per week in 1960.[38] At the time, young women might find work as an assistant in a shop; young men might work as painters and for these types of jobs, might earn between £8 and £10 per week. Taking into account that women traditionally have been paid less than men and that Muriel Day was a teenager at the time, her showband wages were substantial, even at the start of her career.

The ability to earn money was hugely amplified if the performer played in one of the professional bands or, most significantly, moved into the lead position in the band, as was the case with Margo O'Donnell. She began singing in 1964 at the age of 13 in her native Donegal with the Keynotes Showband. Initially a regional band, the Keynotes performed primarily throughout Donegal; as they became better known, they expanded to venues in Ulster, eventually touring Scotland and England. Despite the growing popularity of the band and O'Donnell's happiness working with a group of musicians whom she describes akin to older brothers, she was compelled to leave when a Dublin promoter offered her significantly more money fronting a new band:

I was 16 when my father died [in 1968] … So we didn't have any money. But we were no worse than anybody else because nobody had a lot. I was offered in late '69 £100 a week and a car to take me everywhere. I knew I could look after the rest of [my family]. So I left the Keynotes … they knew that I had to go because of the family, but it broke my heart … I moved to Dublin and then to Galway … [and] I formed Margo and the Country Folk.[39]

Top of the Pops: Negotiating Gender from the Stage

Almost every woman showband artist I spoke with saw herself first as a performing artist who happened to be female rather than as a woman who happened to be on stage. This sense of self contradicts assumptions by audiences and the media, as Helen Davis notes, given that women performers are typically viewed first as female and only secondarily as musicians/performers. The critical repercussion, Davis writes, is the constant stress placed on femininity rather than musicality and performance skills.[40] One of countless examples comes from an article published in the *Dancing Gazette* in December 1966, which features a photograph of Kelley held aloft by her new band-mates in the Big 8 and captioned 'a handful of glamour'. The article describes Kelley first as 'blond' and secondly, as the 'featured vocalist' with the Nevada Showband.[41] Her publicity photos routinely combine this image of the playful fashion icon with vaguely sexually suggestive overtones. In negotiating her role as lead singer in various showbands, Kelley's strategy entailed a certain degree of accommodation and conformity, rather than an insistence on space to be both a woman and performing artist: 'When it's male-dominated like it was … you can still be yourself but you can give a little, as well. I was very good at becoming one of the boys'.[42]

Kelley's approach of simply fitting in allowed her to flourish professionally. Yet, 'becoming one of the boys' also reinforced the very belief systems that limited the role of women in the showband industry in the first place. This borrows from Susan McClary, who, in arguing that because music is always dependent on the conferral of social meaning, it is difficult to not participate without 'unwittingly reproducing the ideologies that inform various levels of this discourse'.[43] Kelley's navigation of both a feminine image in an otherwise masculine context allowed her a measure of professional success, but there was a trade-off. Indeed, the title of the aforementioned article, 'Why Eileen Never Married (But She Says Yes to New Band)', underscores the erroneous assumption concerning the limits of being female and a performer: a woman can marry and have children or she can work in a man's world, but not both.[44] In Kelley's case, the key to success was an embrace of an ultra-feminine playgirl, along with the cultivation of professional competence as a singer and in contrast to the role of woman as wife.[45]

Musically, Kelley made similar strategic choices in carving out her performance niche, preferring contemporary pop songs from the English Top 10 to country and western numbers. She recalls that this focus, along with her ultra-modern stage persona, introduced a new level of sophistication to the Nevada Showband: '[The band] needed somebody who was, I suppose … glamorous … people used to regard me as a sort of a fashion icon'.[46] Her preference for pop music notwithstanding, her manager, George O'Reilly, urged her to also sing country songs, hoping to capitalise on the growing audiences for this genre:

> I never liked country and western, honestly … And I think when George brought me into the band, I think he probably hoped that maybe that's the role that I would take. But I didn't take it; I went into the pop. But if I had to take it in to country and western, I … probably would have done much better.[47]

Muriel Day put similar performance strategies to use to find her place in the showband industry. Like Kelley, Day preferred to sing pop and rock songs. And like Kelley, she looked towards English fashions and music, specifically in the performance and image of the white British soul singer Dusty Springfield. In 1969, Day was the first singer from Northern Ireland to represent the Republic of Ireland in the Eurovision Song Contest, where she finished seventh out of a field of sixteen. She appeared dressed in a modern, bright green mini-dress that fell loosely from her shoulders to the upper thigh, at once modest yet revealing. Thus equating 'the Emerald Isle' with modernity and friskiness, Muriel danced to and sang 'The Wages of Love'. An upbeat pop number, 'The Wages of Love' combines insistent musical enthusiasm with somewhat dour lyrics, cautioning that while love is wondrous, 'When you fall in love, you pay/the wages of love'; and 'There will be bridges to be crossed/ And there'll be teardrops to be lost'.

Performed with exaggerated movements of the arms and hands similar to those of Dusty Springfield, Muriel Day's rendition of 'The Wages of Love' contains some of the melodrama typically found in the 'pop aria', a song type popularised by Springfield in the 1960s. Musicologist Annie Randall characterises the pop aria as 'a short-lived rarefied genre laden with musical and emotional bombast that can only be described as histrionic and shamelessly manipulative'.[48] In mirroring the ethos of Dusty Springfield through the emotionalism of 'The Wages of Love,' coupled with the high energy of pop, Muriel Day's performance was clearly invested in modern sounds and genres. While her performance borrowed heavily from English popular culture, it also semiotically located Ireland in her bright green dress. Muriel Day's performance can be read as an insistence on Irish cultural identity in the simultaneous context of belonging also to a larger, European popular culture.

Singing Country: Articulating Gender on the Stage

Just as women showband artists cast their gaze overseas for pop songs and fashion inspiration, so too did those who preferred country music. They, however, looked not to Britain but to the United States and specifically to Nashville where women recording artists were making their mark. In the United States, country music has long addressed multiple images of femininity through its inclusion of women as performers and as the subject of songs.

Structurally, country music is quite close to Irish musical traditions. Indeed, the birth of early country music and song in the United States was hugely informed by the music and song of Scots-Irish emigrants in the seventeenth century and later.[49] This stylistic overlap explains, in part, the enduring popularity of country music in Ireland. By the mid-twentieth century, country music had emerged as one of the most popular genres of music, thanks to the American Armed Forces Network and Radio Luxembourg, both of which broadcast music for American troops abroad.[50] Country music was so ingrained in Irish popular culture that it was almost mandatory for showbands to include at least some country songs in their repertoire. The 'new Nashville' style of country – one that incorporated pop sounds and instrumentations – in the mid-1960s reinforced this stylistic preference among Irish audiences in the dance halls. Some Irish showbands responded by eliminating their horn sections, adding a fiddle and pedal steel guitar, and revamping their repertoires.

That country music appealed to many women showband performers and their fans is not surprising as it has traditionally presented a range of stereotypes of women captured in song lyrics. Country music scholar Bill Malone notes that feminine imagery embedded in traditional country music ranges from the 'Rough and tough old ladies who are so mean that even the Devil won't take them' to the decidedly more dominant image of women as virtuous, 'the principal quality that men hoped to find in their women'.[51] Many country songs present women as lovers, wives, sisters, and of course, mothers, presenting women as nurturing, down to earth, authentic and whose role it is to reinforce family values.

Country music has historically been somewhat more porous than other popular genres in terms of women's participation and has therefore attracted a range of women artists.[52] The 1950s and 1960s in particular produced a new breed of female Nashville stars such as Jean Shepherd, Kitty Wells, Dolly Parton, and, in particular, Patsy Cline. These vocalists served as models to Irish women singers, some of whom eventually crossed over from showbands to lead country bands.[53] For example, Sandy Kelly moved from the showband world in the 1970s to front a country band, which she felt, unlike pop, gave her more of an authentic voice: 'In a way, turning to country music, for me, was a saviour because I regained my own voice. And being myself. That's why I was so adamant, about being myself'.[54] Sandy Kelly was particularly inspired by the Nashville legend, Patsy Cline; her recording of Patsy Cline's signature hit 'Crazy' in 1989 was Ireland's biggest selling record that year. Kelly remembers that she saw in Patsy Cline both strength and determination in terms of how she managed her career and negotiated her place in the country music industry:

> Patsy Cline was feisty, and cocky and, you know, a woman before her time. I mean, she didn't knock on the door of country music … she kicked the doors down! And when women were window dressing, she was one of the female artists of her time that men were (playing) support to her … For me, as an artist, (sometimes) she'd be there in my mannerisms … I'd put my hand on my hip and say something that I would never say, but it was good, because it'd give me an edge.[55]

Nearly two decades earlier, Margo O'Donnell also crossed over from the showband world into the burgeoning Country and Irish scene. Like Sandy Kelly, she was inspired by Patsy Cline, as both a professional woman and as an artist:

> It was just the quality, the depth, the actual ache [of Patsy Cline's voice]. It was if she was aching the notes. And I … never tried to

sing like anybody, I just sang my own way. But she was my icon: Patsy was a strong woman, she really was. And she was able to stand up for herself.[56]

Margo O'Donnell's own performance style evoked the girl-next-door sensibility, including modest stage outfits and a voice that exuded strength and warmth. Her image combined her working class background with her Donegal roots; as such, O'Donnell personified a rural identity shared by many of her fans. Her own career as one of Ireland's most popular country singers could itself be rendered the subject of a country song. She recorded over forty albums between the mid-1960s through to the 1980s. Her records sold well; indeed, by her own account, in the 1970s, she was selling more records in Ireland than the Beatles. However, O'Donnell never saw a single royalty and she believes that agents, managers and record producers pocketed the profits:

> My life was totally and utterly controlled by gangsters in the music business here … They thought we (women) were second-class citizens. They thought we had no brains. Honest to God, they really thought that it was empty in there and they could do anything they wanted with us. But I'm afraid that's not true.[57]

In 1978, O'Donnell's former manager sold thirty of O'Donnell's master tapes without her knowledge or permission to a Belfast-based producer. The producer then released them for his own profit – even scratch (practice) tracks that were not meant to be heard by the public. O'Donnell took the Belfast producer to court and eventually won the fight to have her master tapes returned:

> I just had to know my own worth … When I heard the judge['s decision] … that day in court, I cried … But I knew [the tapes] were mine … But I … feel as if he raped me … I felt that he had

taken my inside out of me and kicked me along the path of life. And I was not in control of it.[58]

Ireland's popular music industry was all but unregulated with non-existent or vague contracts the norm. All musicians, male and female, were subject to questionable business practices and the absence of written records that documented real income and expenses made it virtually impossible to track profits. As a result, few showband artists were paid royalties for their recordings. The sale and re-release of O'Donnell's master tapes was a particularly pernicious act that severed her from her voice, the ultimate symbolic silencing.

It is tempting to equate the preference of country music by some of these highly successful former showband women singers with notions of tradition and conservatism. Indeed, this coheres neatly with Anne McClintock's argument of 'the temporal anomaly within nationalism – veering between nostalgia for the past and the impatient, sloughing off of the past', such that:

> Women are represented as the atavistic and authentic body of national tradition (inert, backward-looking and natural), embodying nationalism's conservative principle of continuity. Men by contrast, represent the progressive agent of national modernity (forward thrusting, potent and historic) embodying nationalism's progressive, or revolutionary principle of discontinuity.[59]

While performers such as Margo O'Donnell, Philomena Begley, and Sandy Kelly sang country songs that celebrated rural aesthetics, home, locality, community, and family, these women were looking anywhere but backwards. They were in fact radical in their insistence that they not be seen as 'window dressing' and instead, went on to front their own bands. It was also radical to challenge the music industry in a hugely public, civil act, as did Margo O'Donnell, by insisting on gaining control of her music and voice. And, it was radical to simply reject altogether the image of 'girl singer', as Philomena Begley describes 'I just am a singer. I never really went into the nitty-gritty of it, you know what I mean? I would just go out, I would sing, I was just another singer'.[60]

Playing in the (All-Women's) Band

More complex was the case of the few women instrumentalists who found their way into showbands. Occasionally, a woman singer might play guitar or tambourine; otherwise, making music remained very much the purview of male band members. One major exception was Mildred Beirne's all-women five piece, the Granada Girls Showband. This semi-professional showband performed six and even seven nights a week locally and regionally, with an occasional trip to Northern Ireland. The manager, agent and bandleader was musician and arranger Leo Beirne (who Mildred would later marry). Leo Beirne taught the members of the band the music, did the booking, drove them to jobs and served as music director.

Beirne was apparently a strict taskmaster: he insisted on unblemished behaviour when in the public eye, forbidding the girls to leave the stage during breaks or to socialise after the show. He insisted on an absolutely conservative stage appearance where the girls wore matching outfits and always slacks rather than dresses on stage for the sake of propriety. In contrast to the hyper-femininity of many of the other women showband artists, the Granada Girls appear somewhat young and girlish in their publicity photographs, but nevertheless on stage and cheerfully doing, as most audience members saw it, the work of men.

Leo Beirne taught them well and insisted on absolute musical precision; by all reports, the Granada Girls Showband played excellent dance music. So good in fact that patrons initially drawn to the exotic appeal of an all-girl band were surprised at what they found recalls Mildred Beirne:

I'd say that they were taken aback a bit, you know? They couldn't believe that … five women could be as good as we were … I suppose they came thinking that the band mightn't be as good. And instead of that, it was wonderful … They treated us just like queens. We were the belle of the ball. They could not get enough of us.[61]

Mildred Beirne and the Granada Girls Showband clearly were cognisant of the assumptions that their audiences brought with them. While they mastered their instruments and harmony singing and polished their stage performance skills, they were, on some level, trapped in what Christina Baade argues is the 'false binary of male competence and female incompetence'.[62] Irish audiences were attracted to the novelty of an all-women's band but sceptical of their ability to play solid dance music. If women showband vocalists blurred gender codes simply by moving onto the stage, then the Granada Girls as competent instrumentalists and dance musicians pushed the gendered boundaries even further.

For Mildred Beirne, though, being the drummer in the Granada Girls was not so much about gender as it was about the kinetic and psychological pleasure inherent in playing music.

You know when you're a drummer … you're the heart of that band and without the drummer, you can give it up. The drummer gives it everything … For me, it 'twas like magic to sit behind that set of drums and the girls playing. I got lost playing those drums. It was lovely, heaven![63]

Some Conclusions

For musicians like Mildred Beirne, playing in a showband offered a standard of living far removed from what other women in that era might have earned. It also introduced them to the sheer pleasure of performance, a state of mind that arguably transcends gender and offered professional prospects that were all but unheard of in generations past. Finally, playing in a showband presented women with the opportunity to experience a larger and different world and live a broadened lifestyle without having to emigrate. It allowed a personal mobility that engendered possibilities beyond the parochial and familiar for Mildred Beirne and other female showband members in Ireland as Beirne recalls:

> So the band for me, you were taken from nothing to the most wonderful things that could happen to you. You were out every night, playing to all those wonderful dancers on the floor. And like to be on the stage, the people on the dance floor thought we were like angels. And we felt it. And they always made us so welcome and so good and that we were so different.[64]

For showband women, then, the rewards of performance were tempered by challenges ranging from routine indignities to outright exploitation. On a basic level, for most women artists, performing in a showband was fundamentally a job, one that promised not only financial security but also some measure of empowerment. To do this job, women showband artists embedded themselves in the showband world through a variety of strategies — personal, musical and aesthetic — and in doing so blurred gender boundaries at a time when Ireland's popular music industry was just taking shape. Women showband performers thus demonstrated the possibilities of social change and their success would open up future and better opportunities for Irish women pop performers.

4

SEÁN BURKE, LION OF LAHINCH: AN IRA MAN AT THE WALKER CUP

JIM SHANAHAN

As he stood on the first tee of the famous golf course at Brookline, Massachusetts, at the seventh Walker Cup match in September 1932, John Burke of Lahinch may have wondered at the incongruous nature of it all. The Walker Cup pitted the best amateur golfers from Britain against their American counterparts, with the teams selected by the acknowledged governing bodies of the game on both sides of the Atlantic; the United States Golf Association (USGA) and the Royal and Ancient Golf Club of St Andrews (R & A). But John – or Seán – Burke hardly fitted the picture of a typical, not to mention an elite, 'British' amateur golfer. Born on a small farm in west Clare, Burke was still a comparative novice in golfing terms. Four years previously he had shot to prominence virtually overnight when he won the South of Ireland championship at his first attempt. The only Irish player selected for the 1932 match, and only the fourth Irishman ever selected, he was also the first player from the decade-old Irish Free State to be chosen for what was still seen as the 'British' Walker Cup team. There was also, whether it was intended or not, a symbolic element to his selection. As a Catholic from a relatively humble farming background, Burke was much more representative of the population of the Irish Free State than he was of amateur golf in Ireland or elsewhere. Indeed, in the dominant Irish nationalist ethos of the time, the ideal citizen of the Irish Free State was everything the typical elite amateur golfer was not. In choosing Burke, the Walker Cup selectors were perhaps not just making a gesture towards the Irish golfing public, but also the people of the Irish Free State. However, if it was some kind of calculated decision, then even the R & A were surely not aware of just how daring a gesture it was.

If the ability to play golf was the only yardstick employed, then Burke's selection in 1932 was entirely justified. Described by Jack MacGowan in the *Belfast Telegraph* many years later as the 'first of Ireland's golfing legends',[1] Burke was one of a great triumvirate of players, including the better known Joe Carr (captain of Walker Cup teams in 1965 and 1967) and Jimmy Bruen, who dominated amateur golf in Ireland for the first seven decades of the twentieth century. Burke's achievements are undoubtedly in the legendary category. Known as 'The Lion of Lahinch' or 'The King of the South', he was Ireland's most successful amateur golfer in the 1930s and 1940s. He won the 1947 Irish Open Amateur championship and was an eight-time winner of the Irish Close championship in the eighteen years from 1930 to 1947. He was virtually unbeatable in the South of Ireland championship, which was always held on his home course of Lahinch, winning it eleven times between 1928 and 1946. Burke would almost certainly have won it more often during that time if it were not for the fact that he did not participate for much of the 1930s, reputedly at the request of local hoteliers who felt that his dominance of the event was resulting in less golfers coming to compete and subsequently less business for the town.[2] As early as August 1932, the *Clare Champion* reported that 'it is said that the presence of John Burke at the South of Ireland Championship kept many others away'.[3] If one discounts his seven years of self-imposed exile, Burke won the

South of Ireland eleven times in twelve attempts, a truly phenomenal achievement.

Burke also played international golf for Ireland for twenty years; gave putting lessons to the great American golfer, Walter Hagen; and almost incidentally in light of his other achievements, won the West of Ireland championship six times in the first nine years of its inception. He was less successful in the East of Ireland equivalent, finishing runner-up on four occasions after the establishment of that competition in 1940. In 1962 he was the first golfer to be admitted to the Texaco Sports Hall of Fame. All told, he dominated Irish amateur golf for over twenty years from 1928 to 1949. One of the reasons, perhaps, why Burke may not be as well-remembered today as Carr and Bruen is that despite clearly being Ireland's most successful amateur golfer of his own time, he only made that one appearance in the Walker Cup, a match which resulted in a heavy defeat for the British side. Although Burke was one of the best performers on the team, he was never selected again. The fact that Burke never participated in the British Amateur championship was undoubtedly a factor in this, but the traditional reason given for his non-selection – that Burke was reluctant to play outside of Ireland – seems inadequate given that he was an ever-present on the Irish team for internationals between 1929–49; most of which were played outside of Ireland.[4]

To explain this mystery we need to look beyond his individual achievements and to the broader issues of the development of golf in Ireland and Britain, as well as to Burke's own background and personal life. Golf's development as a sport in Britain and Ireland had traditionally reflected the social status quo and provided, as John Lowerson has put it, an opportunity for 'social differentiation, the measurement and assertion of status and the display of achievement and acceptance in the class-ridden world of later Victorian urban life'.[5] Golf had never been, despite Scottish romantic notions of the game's origin, a democratic game, or a game of the people[6] – the cost of participation alone precluded that. Golf's development was driven by a new, increasingly influential and socially ambitious, middle class.[7] In Britain and Ireland it was a game for the establishment and those with aspirations to be part of the establishment. The socially exclusive nature of golf continued to be an important element of the game well into the twentieth century, and continues, albeit in a somewhat less extreme form, to this day. In the Ireland of the late nineteenth and early twentieth century, there were extra religious and political factors to be considered, as the establishment in Ireland tended to be Protestant and unionist, and golf clubs reflected this reality. Unsurprisingly, therefore, golf clubs became a particular target for nationalists and republicans in the first decades of the twentieth century. Burke's own club Lahinch – sometimes called the 'St Andrews of Ireland' – was founded in 1892 by the wealthy landed and merchant classes of Limerick (notably the Shaw family) and was, as most golf clubs were then, firmly associated with the establishment and the military. Golf clubs were the preserve of the gentry and the influential. The Black Watch regiment, a detachment of which were then based in Limerick, were also instrumental in the founding of the Lahinch club. They were bastions of political conservatism (and, in Ireland, unionism) in the early decades of the twentieth century.

Golf was first formally played at Lahinch on 15 April 1892. Appropriately, that first game was between a Lieutenant McFarlane of the Black Watch and a Mr William McDonnell, a Limerick businessman.[8] The opening ceremonies included the raising of the Union flag and a toast to the king. The very fact that the first game was played on Good Friday, and that meat was prominent on the menu for the post-ceremony celebrations, is indication enough of the difference between the visiting golf party and the vast majority of the population of Lahinch and its environs. It was some years later before membership of the club was open to locals and even then only prominent local businessmen were considered for membership. Lahinch was in effect the summer golf location for the members of Limerick Golf Club. A flick through the pages of the society magazines, *Irish Life* or the *Irish Field* – not to mention the very existence of a publication such as *The Irish Golfer* – in this period demonstrates the level to which golf was synonymous with the landed gentry, the business classes and political conservatism. Golf clubs such as The Island in Malahide, for example, operated a highly exclusive membership policy. Daniel Mulhall, in an article on golf's early days in Ireland, cites the memoirs of the journalist and broadcaster Brian Inglis, who recalled that it was not enough just to be a Protestant to obtain membership of The Island, but you had to have an impeccable – that is, a landed – social background.[9] Mulhall's view that it was 'tempting to see Ireland's golf clubs as places to which the Anglo-Irish elite retreated in the decades following the fall of Parnell to enjoy a final *belle époque* before war and revolution brought their long period of social ascendancy to an end', is difficult to disagree with.[10] What this suggests is that the development of golf in Ireland differed only in local nuance from the way it evolved in Scotland and England. It was a game for the elite, played by the elite, in the company of other members of the elite. Golf clubs were, as Richard Holt observes with regard to the new golf clubs of suburban England, 'worlds within worlds, business contacts and mutual reassurance for the reasonably well off, islands of sociability within the unfathomable seas of domestic privacy'.[11] In an Irish context one could add politics and religion to this mix. In the Ireland of the first decades of the twentieth century, golf was associated with the political and social status quo, which meant political conservatism, the British army, and unionism.

Committed Irish nationalists, not to mention hard-core republicans, therefore, had good historical and political reasons not to be attracted to the game of golf, even if the opportunity to play the game presented itself. General histories of golf in Ireland tend to avoid political issues, but, as Patrick Maume has observed, there is evidence to suggest that the depth of general nationalist antipathy to golf may be underestimated.[12] Many nationalists had objections to golf both because of its connections with class and social snobbery and because of its association with unpopular conservative politicians such as Arthur Balfour, who was chief secretary of Ireland in the 1880s and a self-styled ambassador of golf. Known as 'Bloody Balfour' by nationalists, during his time in Ireland Balfour used to play golf under heavy police protection on a specially constructed course in the Phoenix Park. The course itself was eventually the subject of an attack by Land League activists. Another prominent golfer unpopular with nationalists was Andrew Bonar Law, who succeeded Balfour as leader of the Conservative party in 1911. Interestingly, golf was never included in the GAA's list of banned games, possibly because it was not in direct competition with any of their games and perceived to be of 'Celtic' origin. Nonetheless, even after the establishment of the Free State, golf clubs continued to be places of social privilege and golfers came largely from the more affluent and influential social classes. Indeed, golf clubs may even have grown in importance as places where like-minded individuals could meet and socialise together.[13]

In this context, therefore, John Burke was the most unlikely of golf heroes. In contrast to many of the top amateur golfers of his era, Burke was a working man. He was born in Moybeg, near Ennistymon in County Clare, in 1899, one of a large family born to Patrick and Mary Burke, who had a small farm. He was obviously a clever child: educated at the local national school in Moy, he reputedly obtained a scholarship to train as a teacher, but for some reason turned down the opportunity. As a young boy, he used to caddy at the local Lahinch club with his friend Mick O'Loughlin – who also became a stalwart of the club and a two-time South of Ireland winner – and tradition has it that the pair used to play illegally on the course when the opportunity presented itself. Family sources suggest that Burke eventually bought a couple of golf clubs in Clerys' department store on a rare trip to Dublin, and his unorthodox playing style and ability to pull off incredible shots when required was often ascribed to the fact that Burke mastered the game with an extremely limited number of clubs.[14]

Perhaps the most remarkable aspect of Burke's golfing career, however, is the fact that he was nearly thirty years of age before he began to play the game seriously. Burke's friend Ivan Morris suggests that Burke and O'Loughlin became members of Lahinch in April 1928 at the insistence of a far-sighted incoming captain, William O'Dwyer.[15] What is certain is that the following September Burke won the South of Ireland championship at the first attempt. Such was Burke's swift rise to the top of amateur golf that in 1932 American journalists, never having seen him but aware of his sudden arrival on the golf scene, assumed that he was 'a youngster'.[16] Burke's victory in the 'South' in 1928 was to be the first of four wins in a row stretching to 1931. He was also Irish Close, or 'Native' champion in four consecutive years, from 1930 to 1933. Burke was the first local who was not a businessman to be admitted to the still-exclusive Lahinch club. Apart from farm work in early adulthood, family sources assert that Burke may have worked with a brother in a local sawmill, and that he was later in insurance, but the *Clare Champion* in 1932 reported that he had formerly been a rate collector – a somewhat less popular occupation than an insurance salesman – and that he had recently been appointed to a position with a Limerick oil and petrol distributor.[17] Piecing together Burke's pre-golf years is not a straightforward task. One reason is that as a young man he eloped to Limerick with Nora Sexton, a local girl, where they married in 1922. Additionally, during the War of Independence Burke had been a member of the fourth battalion of the Mid-Clare brigade of the IRA, further contributing to vagueness about his past.

Burke's first involvement with the South of Ireland Championship came in a political rather than a sporting context. In 1920 Burke was reputedly one of a number of local IRA activists who took down and burned the Union flag flying at the Championship and replaced it with the Irish tricolour.[18] Later that September, Burke, with his brother Tom and several other local men from Ennistymon, took part in one of the most notorious incidents in the War of Independence: an ambush at

Rineen in County Clare, in which six RIC men were killed. Eye-witness testimony suggests that Burke was one of four riflemen whose role in the ambush was to pick off anyone who escaped from the ambushed tender.[19] The Rineen ambush provoked an immediate and deadly response from the RIC, when later that night they engaged in a reprisal action in Ennistymon, Lahinch and Miltown Malbay, killing six local people, including a 12-year-old boy. These two incidents effectively brought an end to the War of Independence in west Clare.[20] But it was another incident during the War of Independence that ultimately sowed the seeds for his Walker Cup undoing as Burke saw it. In a story told years later to Ivan Morris, Burke recounted an incident when, as the result of a raid by his brigade on a British army encampment in County Cork, he serendipitously obtained a pair of boots with the initials 'JB', which obviously belonged to an officer with the same initials as himself. Some weeks later, when Burke was detained for questioning in Clare, he gradually realised that the boots he was then wearing belonged to the interrogating officer. As Morris writes: 'It could have been disastrous if it had been discovered. Fortunately for [Burke], a most uncomfortable few hours passed by without the boots being noticed.'[21] This story takes an even more extraordinary turn as apparently, some years later, when Burke was playing for Ireland against England in the 'home' internationals, he met that same officer, who was at the match as a spectator, and struck up a friendship with him. It was this chance occurrence that would have implications for his Walker Cup career.[22]

Burke was not the first Irishman to be selected for the Walker Cup. Depending on which source you choose to credit, he was either the third or fourth Irishman to be selected; the definition of who was 'Irish' being complicated by issues of place of birth and residence, as well as by wider and more nebulous factors such as political loyalty, religion and ethnicity, particularly in the context of a recently divided island. The *Irish Times*, a dependably conservative source in the circumstances, listed him as the fourth Irishman to be picked after Major Charles O. (known as

'C.O.H'.) Hezlet – one of the famous Hezlet golfing family from Royal Portrush in County Antrim – Major G.N.C. (Noel) Martin and the Hon. W. Brownlow.[23] Hezlet and Martin were members of the Royal Portrush club, later rising to the ranks of Lieutenant Colonel and Brigadier General respectively, and both won the DSO and MC. Interestingly, another Irishman, J.D. McCormack, had initially been selected for the 1926 match, but as a Medical Officer with the Free State's Department of Local Government, his superiors refused to grant him leave of absence to compete. This was perhaps indicative of official attitudes in the new Free State at the time. The social and professional status of Burke's three predecessors serves as a reminder of the incongruity of Burke's selection.

Burke is sometimes referred to as the first 'Irish-based' player to be picked, and this also reveals something of the contentious nature of the term 'Irish' and the lifestyles of Burke's Irish Walker Cup predecessors. His inclusion was not only striking a blow for the working man in general, but was doubly delicate as he was also the first player from the Irish Free State to compete. The *Times*, keeping its cards close to its chest, expressed the view that Burke was a 'dark horse', but also admitted that 'no one in the eight [chosen players] was likely to play more winning shots'.[24] The *doyen* of English golfing journalists, Bernard Darwin, who had played in the Walker Cup himself, struck a similar note, and was quoted as saying that Burke 'lives rather out of the world and cannot get away much', but he 'has the whole game in him and can be surpassingly brilliant', before asserting that he had seen Burke play 'one of the best rounds I had ever seen played by an amateur'.[25] Coming from Darwin, this was praise indeed. Living 'rather out of the world and cannot get away much' can be seen as a polite way of saying that Burke lived in a remote Irish location and had a day job to keep down. This was clearly seen as an issue and the *Clare Champion* was of the opinion that, in order to do himself justice, he needed more opportunities to compete. Burke himself admitted that it was difficult in the circumstances to get good-quality practice, especially, as he euphemistically put it, when you have 'interests in life other than golf'.[26] Luckily, the opportunity for practice presented itself. There had been some criticism of previous Walker Cup teams' lack of preparation, and a practice session for the team at St Andrews in Scotland was arranged shortly before they left for America. Burke was clearly a novelty for the wider golfing public: the *Clare Champion* reported that their local man was very popular in Scotland and his autograph – which he always signed in Irish – was 'in great demand by autograph hunters'.[27]

But Burke's novelty value also has to be considered in the wider context of Anglo-Irish relations of the early 1930s, which at this time were still difficult. The Free State was in the midst of a financial crisis, and the Land Annuities issue was coming to a head. The same issue of the *Clare Champion* that described Burke's experiences in Scotland also reported that a motion proposing a ban on British goods being purchased by Limerick Corporation was passed unanimously by that body. In addition, there was still sporadic republican violence in Burke's native Clare. The year 1932 saw an attempted murder and a bombing in the county, and an inquiry into the activities of the Gardaí and republicans in County Clare was the major news item in the local papers. Against this background of persistent tension within the Free State and in the Free State's relationship with Britain, it is not difficult to see why Burke's selection for the Walker Cup was interpreted by the *Irish Independent* as an optimistic sign, and was referred to rather pointedly as a 'British gesture'.[28]

The Great Britain team left for America on Saturday, 13 August 1932 and upon arrival in the USA, Burke immediately hit good form. In a practice round held at Brookline on 22 August, Burke posted the best score, going around in 68. Four days later he also posted the best practice score of the British team, recording a 70. The *Irish Times* reported that Burke was 'extremely popular with the players of each country and the spectators who follow the practice rounds'.[29] A few days later, the paper stated that Burke was playing 'excellent golf', a judgement confirmed by the fact that the British captain, T.A. (Tony) Torrance, selected Burke to play alongside the experienced J.A. Stout in the second of the opening foursomes matches. The day didn't go well for them, or the British team, however. Burke and Stout lost the first four holes and were five down after fourteen, eventually losing by 7 and 6 on the thirtieth hole of the scheduled 36-hole match, and the British team lost all four matches to the Americans.

Burke and Stout's heavy defeat has to be put in the context that they were facing the USA's best players: the American captain, Francis Ouimet, a Brookline local and the 1931 US Amateur Champion; and George Dunlap, who would win that title in 1933. Ouimet was the most famous American amateur of the time, and one of the most important figures in the history of American golf. In 1913 he had sensationally won the US Open, defeating the best professional players, including the legendary English golfer, Harry Vardon, in a tournament regarded as having transformed the profile of golf in the USA.[30] Ouimet would act as captain of the US Walker Cup team on six more occasions. Facing one of the giants of the American game could not have been anything other than the most intimidating of prospects. Interestingly, Burke probably had more in common with Ouimet than with any other player at that Walker Cup. Ouimet was born into a poor family, and he initially made a start in golf working as a caddy at Brookline, just as Burke did at Lahinch, before his enormous talent ensured that he could not be ignored. Even more coincidentally, perhaps, Ouimet's mother was an Irish emigrant's daughter named Mary Burke: the same name as Burke's own mother. Despite this crushing defeat, Burke managed to rally in the singles the following day. Playing in the seventh match against Jack Westland, the 1931 US Amateur runner-up, Burke came back from being three down with three holes to play, securing a half when he played a beautiful shot out of a bunker to within a few centimetres of the hole on the eighteenth.[31] The British team, however, was generally outclassed, and comfortably defeated by 9½ to 2½.

So much for the official account of the Brookline match. Although the British team was heavily defeated, Burke was far from being the worst performer, and there was little in his playing performance to explain why he was subsequently ignored by the Walker Cup selectors. From the British perspective it was acknowledged that the team had been well beaten, but it was also noted that the American captain Ouimet had putted exceptionally well against Burke and Stout in the foursomes, and that Torrance, Stout and Burke had all 'recovered nobly from very gloomy situations in the singles'.[32] Burke's own explanation for his subsequent failure to be selected for the Walker Cup again is revealed in the account he gave to Ivan Morris in the latter's book *Only Golf Spoken Here* (2001). Burke claims that his IRA past came to light while the team was in transit to America, and it was made clear to him that while the authorities could not prevent his participation on this occasion, he would under no circumstances be considered for future teams.[33] Morris writes that Burke was treated as *persona non grata* by his colleagues on the trip, and that he retaliated by refusing to honour the British national anthem and insisting on having his Irish nationality recognised at every opportunity.[34] If this is true, then it is not difficult to see why Burke was never picked again.

It is also difficult, however, to verify this particular version of events. Understandably perhaps, there is no hint of controversy in the newspapers of the time. *The Times*, commenting on reports from the Brookline course on the British team's practice rounds wrote, 'It has been particularly pleasant to read that Mr Burke has been playing brilliant rounds in practice. The choosing of him was regarded, not unjustly perhaps, as something of a gamble, but no one who has seen him at his best can doubt his real quality'. The report concludes with the comment, 'I only hope he has not, as the Americans say, "shot his head off" in those preliminary 68's'.[35] Given Burke's IRA past, this can be seen as either an unfortunate turn of phrase in the circumstances, or a knowing wisecrack. Burke's much-reported popularity with his fellow players does seem to be at odds with his portrayal of himself as *persona non grata*. However, it is clear that not everything that occurred at that Walker Cup was reported in the media. Gordon Simmonds's semi-official history of the competition reports that two of the British team, disappointed with the side's showing on the first day, elected to sample the local nightlife instead of attending the singles matches on the second day. These were the Scot J.T. Bookless, who had played badly in the foursomes and John de Forest, then the holder of the British Amateur title, whose poor form in practice meant that he did not play any part in the match. It is also possible, of course, that Burke's nationalistic protestations were more low-key than those he recalled some three decades later. Simmonds' book makes no mention of any incidences in connection with Burke. In fact, conspiracy theorists can probably take something out of the fact that Burke doesn't rate a mention at all, except in the statistics. It seems that Burke has not so much been expunged as simply ignored in Walker Cup history.[36]

There are definite discrepancies in Burke's story as told by Morris. Morris writes that Burke's IRA involvement came to light when his British army friend went to Southampton to see the team off. According to Morris, the officer did not realise that Burke was joining up with the team when the Queen Mary called at Cobh, and, not seeing Burke, he asked a Royal and Ancient (R&A or Golf Club of St Andrews) official to pass on a note wishing Burke the best of luck. In this version of the story, Burke's friend and the official got chatting and Burke's IRA past was revealed.[37] However, the *Times* states that the team left not from Southampton on the Queen Mary, but from Liverpool on the Britannia, and Burke's name is listed as being among the travelling party.[38] The only team members listed absent were P.W. Hartley and the seemingly free-spirited de Forest, who had left for America on an earlier liner. At this remove, the newspaper report seems much more likely. The team, after all, had been in Scotland practicing at St Andrews and it seems more logical to leave from Liverpool rather than travel all the way down to Southampton. More importantly, it seems unlikely that Burke would travel all the way back to Ireland from Scotland just to rejoin the team in Cobh. If Burke was on the liner in Liverpool as the *Times* reports, then it casts some considerable doubt over the story about the British officer being the catalyst for his IRA past being revealed. The only R&A official listed as travelling with the team from Liverpool was the R&A secretary, Henry Gullen.[39] If Burke's British army friend had talked to anyone it was most likely to him.

Undoubtedly, the secretary of the R&A, under whose auspices the Walker Cup team was selected, would have been a powerful enemy for any golfer, but as to Burke's subsequent non-selection for Walker Cup teams, it is worth noticing that only four of the ten players selected in 1932 were selected again in 1934. If there was a ban, official or unofficial, on Burke, the *Times* does not appear to have been aware of it. Commenting on the players not selected in 1934, Burke is mentioned as a player that 'many believe to be worth his place'.[40] Two years later, the 1936 team contained only two players with previous Walker Cup experience and they were subsequently crushed 9-0. In 1938 trials took place for the first time and 25 players were invited to try out for the team, but Burke was not one of them. After that, the war intervened and there were no further Walker Cups until 1947, Burke's last great year as a competitive player.

Was Burke banned, officially or unofficially, from the Walker Cup? The most obvious evidence on the 'no' side lies in the fact that he actually played in 1932 after his background was supposedly revealed. Torrance, the captain, had ten players to choose from and he could have left him out entirely. It is possible, though, that Burke's blinding form in practice and the obviously poor form of others (i.e. de Forest) may have forced the selectors' hand. The heavy 7 and 6 defeat in the foursomes might have provided some excuse to drop him, but it is possible that the nocturnal activities of Bookless and de Forest may have left the selectors with no choice but to play Burke in the singles. Other circumstantial evidence on the 'no' side lies in the fact that the R&A selectors in the 1930s seemed to be engaged in a policy of selecting new talent and there was a high turnover of players from one Walker Cup to another. The British team was consistently heavily beaten by the Americans and few players, perhaps, deserved to keep their place. The nature of the selection process for much of this period seems unscientific, partial and haphazard to modern eyes, and probably contributed to Britain's poor performance and therefore, a high turnover of players from match to match. It was only in 1938, when the team was selected after extensive trials, that Britain finally won the Walker Cup for the first time. Another reason why Burke could have been ignored is the fact that the period 1933–39 coincided with Burke's most barren time in terms of victories in major competitions – if by 'barren' we mean merely two National Close titles, four West of Ireland and one South of Ireland title – and coincided with his self-imposed exile from the South of Ireland competition. In addition, his reluctance – or, due to work commitments, his unavailability – to participate in the major British competitions may not have helped his profile.

Looking at the selection process overall, there seems little doubt that preference was given to players who regularly competed in the major British competitions and, perhaps, to Scottish and English players in general. Burke was not the first Irish player to be inexplicably ignored by Walker Cup selectors. Captain Ernest Carter of Royal Portrush missed out on selection for the very first Walker Cup team in 1922, despite being regarded as a certainty for selection. Carter's social status and background were impeccable in this regard, although there was some question mark over his involvement with some golfing equipment manufacturers.[41] Possible discrimination on nationality or class grounds may have affected Burke, but this is not the same as being banned for being an ex-IRA man. The fact that he was not one of the 25 called for a trial for the 1938 team might appear to suggest that he was *persona non grata*, but contemporary newspaper reports stated that the team was not necessarily going to be picked from the 25 trialists, and that other players, whose track record was known (and Burke was surely one of these) would be considered.[42] In addition, it appears that the British selectors generally attempted to pick teams to suit the course on which the competition was to be played – although with little apparent effect on results, as we have seen. Lastly, the discrepancies in the only recorded version of his story and the lack of written evidence to corroborate it would lead a historian to doubt its veracity, or at least to suggest that it may have been one of those stories that, as they say, grew in the telling.

On the other hand, an unofficial ban is the most obvious reason why a golfer of his undoubted ability could be so consistently and completely ignored, particularly in the context of regular and comprehensive defeats by the Americans. More tellingly, perhaps, the fact that other Irish players – Lionel Munn, Cecil Ewing and a young Jimmy Bruen, to name but three – were picked ahead of him in the 1930s also suggests that Burke, the most successful of them all at the time, was ignored or disregarded for some specific reason. Form cannot be the issue as he remained highly competitive right up to the end of his career. Indeed, 1947 was probably Burke's finest year: he won the Irish Close championship for the eighth and final time, the last of his eleven South of Ireland titles and the Irish Open Amateur title for the first and only time. In addition, although some of the details of his own story as reported by Ivan Morris appear to be incorrect, this may not have been deliberate. He may have recollected them incorrectly, or they may have been recorded inaccurately – it would be quite easy to make the assumption that they left from Southampton on the Queen Mary, for example. Burke was a great raconteur, and, given the clubbable nature of golf, it would be quite easy for a story to grow in the telling for entertainment purposes and still be substantially true. William Menton describes Burke as 'an imaginative story teller' who would 'liberally embellish some of his reminiscences to suit his different audiences'.[43] This might lead one to disregard Burke's account of events as a tall tale told for the entertainment of listeners at the nineteenth hole, but Burke's IRA past was genuine and widely-known, and it seems inconceivable that the golfing establishment would not have become aware of it eventually. While his 1932 experience may not have happened quite as it is described in Morris's book, it does not preclude the possibility that he was quietly ignored subsequently by Walker Cup selectors.

Taking everything into consideration the most likely scenario is that Burke's past did come to light at some stage, possibly during the trip to America, that it was disapproved of by the golfing establishment, and that this, allied to his non-participation in the British Amateur Championship resulted in Burke being quietly and consistently ignored. So what should we make of John Burke and his Walker Cup adventure and what does it say about Burke, golf and Anglo-Irish relations in the 1930s? Burke has to be seen, as a working man and an active Irish nationalist, as a pioneer of sorts in the field of golf, both in this country and in British golf circles. Like many pioneers, however, Burke may also have been a victim. While he was unusual (but not unique) in Irish golf terms, he was perhaps unthinkable in terms of British golfing politics.[44] In the end, rather than focusing on the perceived inflexibility or intolerance of the British golfing establishment, it is more interesting to reflect on the remarkable fact that a man, who had been an active member of the IRA during the War of Independence, was, just over a decade later, prepared to play for a team essentially representing Great Britain. Most of all perhaps, and considering the issue on a personal rather than a political level, it seems simply a shame that the golfer described by the great Fred Daly as 'the finest natural golfer I've ever set eyes upon', only played once in the Walker Cup.[45]

5 CORNER BOYS IN SMALL TOWN IRELAND, 1922–1970

LEO KEOHANE

Introduction

When Joyce wrote to his agent Grant Richards outlining his aims for *Dubliners,* he declared 'my intention was to write a chapter in the moral history of my country and I chose Dublin for the scene because that city seemed to me the centre of paralysis.'[1] Despite its burgeoning literary and cultural revival, the fading of the horrors of famine, and the promise of home rule indicating an end to the miseries of revolution, land wars and emigration, Joyce saw an anomie pervading Irish society that would require more than independence to alleviate.

Whether the seeds of recovery began after 1922, or the patient had a further relapse does not take from the point that the period from independence until 1970 was a particularly conservative one. Various governments during that time collaborated with, or were unduly influenced by, vociferous minorities whose zeal in advocating a sexual Puritanism was rivalled only by their sacral nationalism. This was a moral and political climate where a white paper on censorship was entitled 'Report of the Committee on Evil Literature' and Kathleen Kirwan, a witness before the Carrigan Committee (1930–1) suggested that extramarital sex should be made a criminal offence.[2] Kirwan, not shy of also establishing her nationalist credentials, wrote a pamphlet entitled, *Towards Irish Nationalism: A Tract: Offered in Awe and Reverence to the Sublime Patience and Agonised Endurance of the Exploited People of Ireland.*[3]

Of course, while there were voices of opposition, there were also positive aspects to this conservative society. At the least there must have been a sense of security after the depredations of the Black and Tans and the Civil War. There was stability in government and if de Valera's cosy fireside and dancing maidens were an idealistic piece of nonsense, many would have felt that the traumatising and de-eroticising of sexuality described in Kavanagh's contemporaneous *The Great Hunger* was either exaggerated or a price worth paying. What is of relevance is the prevailing atmosphere of the times, that is, a prudishness coupled with a censorious interference into what might be imagined elsewhere to be matters of private concern only.

John McGahern, who lost his teaching job in 1965 as a result of a perceived transgression of the mores of that period, never adopted an embittered stance but, for all that, said it was 'not too crude to say that Church and State had colluded to bring about a climate that was insular, repressive, sectarian'.[4] He maintained that 'the country was being run almost exclusively for a small Catholic middle class and its church' but more importantly wrote that 'the whole holy situation … was of our own making. Britain could no longer be blamed'. Whether 'of our own making' was ever accepted by the various dominant groups of the time is questionable. Nationalism, and a Catholic brand at that, was the bread and circuses that maintained the elite in its elevated position in both the secular and religious hierarchies.

Nonetheless, people had to live and love, and hope and work, and rear children and engage in the rites and practices of living and dying in that period. If the proscriptions and regulations of the authorities were enthusiastically supported by a vociferous minority, there was a substantial, though complacent, majority that might not have believed or accepted these strictures. McGahern, a little fancifully, said 'that most people were untouched by all this and went about their sensible pagan lives as they had done for centuries, seeing it as one of the many veneers they had to pretend to wear like all the others worn since the time of the Druids'.[5] Anthony Cronin makes a more pointed aside, 'so holy was Ireland then and so strangely afraid ….'[6]

Although Althusser's notion of the Ideological State Apparatus is a little dated, one of its basic premises that ideologies are what keep the general populace in line with the dictates of the state, is still valid.[7] Importantly, for this to work efficiently the pressure of government needs to be assuaged from time to time, hence, a healthy scepticism among a large number of the hoi polloi about banners of allegiance needs to be permitted to be expressed. The Rabelaisian *Carnival* with its inversion of hierarchies and values allows for this, and among its many manifestations are practices and beliefs that arise and form part of the underbelly of a people's outlook. These activities alleviate the inevitable tensions that result from the repressiveness of a regime and have the tacit, but covert, support of the authorities. Covert, because an obvious approval from the state would detract from and devalue the perceived subversive behaviour.

To be more specific, an innocuous example, little remembered and quite local, was the evasion of the imposed dietary restrictions around Lenten times. When the authoritarian Bishop of Cork (1951–1980), Cornelius Lucey, decreed that the Lenten Fast could be broken by one full meal and a collation, he defined the collation as tea and a biscuit. This gave rise to very large pieces of confectionery known locally as 'Conny Dodgers'.[8] An innocent term that will never rank among the great banners in the annals of revolution but, nevertheless, drew some of the venom that a grumbling stomach would cause. It also formed part of the popular discourse of that period. That is, a discourse that arose from the quotidian activities of the populace, of which a large part involved coming to terms with, if not exactly coping with, the interferences of the authorities.

This paper proposes that another phenomenon with subversive connotations, the small town 'corner boy', was a more general and more visible representation of that popular discourse. Although it is a term that had been used for over one hundred and fifty years, its meaning has changed over time and in the period 1920 to 1970, it was generally understood as a relatively innocuous group of male layabouts who gathered in strategic places, mainly the corners, of small towns. This discussion is less concerned with what corner boys were, rather than what they represented in the eyes of the general public and it addresses, to some extent, various aspects of the behaviour and possible outlook of these people. The argument is that 'corner boy/s' was a trope that fulfilled a need in the vocabulary of the popular parlance; it expressed some part of the outlook of a community. And what this was, was redolent of the times, the specific *episteme* so to speak, that existed in Ireland over those fifty years – a time of sententious disapproval.

Origins of the Phrase

The *Oxford English Dictionary* (*OED*) traces the earliest usage of the term 'corner boy' to c.1855, contemporaneous with 'corner coves'. At that time it was used to describe thugs who lay in wait for unsuspecting travellers along the street and alleyways of urban areas. Although there were plenty of street criminals in England and Scotland the dictionary emphasises its specifically Irish connotations from the beginning. It quotes the *Standard* in 1882 referring to 'the Dublin loafers or "corner boys" as they're called'. Ironically, the term commonly used in England, although later, was hooligan. This is generally acknowledged to be of Irish origin, probably from a mispronunciation of the surname Houlihan.[9]

In a trawl through the *Irish Times* and the *Times*, the phrase 'corner boy' appears nearly five hundred times from 1850 up to the present day in the Irish paper. The phrase was found less than a hundred times in the English paper and then almost invariably referring to some situation in Ireland. It seems there is no direct equivalent of corner boy in the Irish language[10], suggesting that this is an original product of Hiberno-English, that is, a cultural concept peculiar to this island, and a relatively modern one at that.

To judge by the newspaper reports of the time, the streets of Dublin in the mid-nineteenth century were particularly violent and dangerous places. The term 'corner boy' was freely employed to describe the miscreants and criminals of that time and was severely pejorative. Towards the end of the century, possibly as the level of street violence diminished, or, as the level of reporting decreased, the term itself lost some of its edge and began to be used more often as a political jibe. John Redmond complained that his opponents claimed there was 'no one on his side except drunken rowdies and corner-boys' and the Parnellites became almost synonymous with the term.[11]

Interestingly, today it features as one of the descriptions that is not allowed in the Dáil when referring to one's opponents.[12] Despite this the columnist Ronald Quinlan remarked that in Bertie Ahern there 'lurks a Drumcondra corner boy'; although this is probably an illustration of how the term has even further lost its derogatory sting and could even suggest (at a stretch, I admit) a modicum of affection.[13] However, there is little affection in Professor Mahaffy's purported dismissal of Joyce as one who was 'a living argument in favour of my contention that it was a mistake to establish a separate university for the aborigines of this island – for the corner boys who spit in the Liffey'.[14] Although Professor W.B. Stafford, one of the biographers of Mahaffy, maintained that he never made this remark,[15] Joyce himself regularly attracted this appellation; there was something about him of the smart alec with a fund of sardonic comments on humankind. Desmond Rushe, approvingly it seems, quotes Dr. John Garvin calling Joyce an 'intellectual corner boy preoccupied with the obscene'.[16]

The first sporting greyhound named Corner Boy appeared in 1881 and thereafter there have been at least half a dozen other animals, including several decent racehorses.[17] Oddly, 'corner-boy' appears in crossword clues in *The Times* on at least seven different occasions. This forms about eight per cent of the entire strike for the term over one hundred and fifty years in the English paper, and in this particular case they appear from 1939 to 1970 – a mere thirty years.[18] What this indicates is the essential ambiguity of the term and its attraction to other types of discourse. Etymologically, 'corner boy' has gradually evolved from denotations of brigandage and criminality in the mid-nineteenth century to disparaging politicians around the time of Parnell. By the 1930s, 'corner boys' was being used to describe a collection of men who gathered at strategic interstices in various towns and who were generally innocuous if not downright useless from the point of view of any conventional criteria.

These then are the people I wish to discuss and I believe that particular type flourished, if one could use such an inappropriate term, from the 1920s to the late 1960s. It is not the intention of this essay to define them much more closely than that. It is rather a discourse on the manifestation of corner boys in Ireland and as such is concerned with what the corner boys represented rather than any indisputable analysis of what they were composed. In fact, corner boys are a nebulous concept and their ephemeral existence is particularly appropriate to the liminal space they occupied in their small communities. Probably the rhetorical term, antonomasia, technically indicates the point being made; this is a 'naming instead', the use of a word or phrase to express a more complicated concept – Casanova for a libidinously inclined male, for example. Here it is hoped to demonstrate that the phrase was a signifier for something more considerable than a group of men gathering to pass the time. On the other hand, to call them a 'conceit' might be a step too far; although originally a synonym for thought, it nowadays denotes 'a fanciful supposition', more within the remit of poetic discourse than to be employed about a collective whose lowly status was particularly pertinent.[19] The corner boys' demise, or more correctly their disappearance, occurred around the late 1960s and this is rather satisfyingly marked by the *Irish Times* which conveniently for this chapter decided, in their weekly literary competition in 1975, to commemorate their end:

> A Vanished Species. Where has the corner-boy gone? Account for the extinction in a suitable threnody. A very large entry … There was inevitable repetition and begging everyone's pardon – far too rosy a view of the type.[20]

The winning entry, by Liam Brophy, quite perceptively suggested that the corner-boy had 'become the many mouthed mass, The seething human sum, Unclassified new class'.[21] Those occupants of the liminal, no longer required, or of benefit, had vanished and with them the term itself fell out of use.

What did they do (if anything)?

William Desmond writes that '"Being Between" is perhaps the central concern of [his] philosophical work' and uses his neologism *metaxologia* to describe his existence after a diasporic career between Ireland, America and Louvain in Belgium. His experience of two homes was that 'these two worlds could never be reduced to a unity'; he was *idir eatarthu*. Extending this to his being 'haunted' by the Irish tongue he suggests that, in a more general fashion, the *metaxological* might be 'of aid in articulating some Irish conditions?'[22]

Similarly, I would argue that the corner boy also articulates some Irish outlook, and as with Desmond himself, the corner boys were also, geographically, in a between space. Neither urban or rural denizens of the small towns; neither at home or abroad, standing all day on street corners; and neither traditional or modern, occupying a liminal space that is neither forward or backwards, past or future, they were, literally, men of metaxologia. What they articulated is not as easily answered. Their position in the hierarchical structure of these communities was lowly, but did their occupation of such a strategic location infer obligations on their part? Was their tacit acceptance by other residents an indication that they might perform some duties in reciprocation? Or was it merely a holding point by the community for citizens, exclusively male, whose position as drones in a beehive would have resulted in their summary disposal? Was their continued toleration by the rest of the community evidence of a benignity previously unsuspected in small towns?

Were they waiting for Godot? Desultory though the stage characters are drawn, it is suggested that, paraphrasing the old joke, a degree of urgency underlined the play that was distinctly missing from our subjects. Beckett's genius was in the depiction of the universal human condition; the corner boy was more of an exceptional character and although he was no more free of the conventional anxieties and delusions of life, it is not what marks him out for special attention. Could comparisons be drawn between them and the continental *flaneurs*? Although obviously of a stationary type, would, more significantly, their bucolic lack of sophistication disqualify them? Theorists of popular culture would protest that their perceptions and sensitivities would be just as valid as the Baudelairean observer. Still, it would be the rare small town corner boy who would be found to respond thus:

> A woman passed, raising, with dignity
> In her poised hand, the flounces of her gown;
> Graceful, noble, with a statue's form.
> And I drank, trembling as a madman thrills.[23]

Of course, the *flaneur* moved along the boulevards and had a continual change of scenery but staying in one place probably guaranteed that one missed less in the sense that everything eventually passed by anyway. Walter Benjamin sees three types of 'gentlemen of leisure' participating in these activities. There is the London 'man of the crowd' (probably interchangeable with Chesterton's man on the Clapham omnibus); interestingly there is the Berlin street corner boy 'Nante ... a popular figure in Berlin before the March Revolution of 1848' and, thirdly, the Parisian *flaneur* who 'might be said to stand midway between them'. He states that 'the man of the crowd is no *flaneur*. In him composure has given way to manic behaviour'.[24] In other words, I would suggest, the boulevardier was a neutral: he merely observed. The corner boy at least commented and, more importantly, it is argued later, influenced with his gaze.

John B. Keane suggested that the corner boys represented a Greek chorus, who were 'never part of the scene, except in a spiritual sense'.[25] H.D.F. Kitto maintains that in the earlier plays of Aeschylus 'an atmosphere of vengeance and retribution [and] ... the background of doom and battle, are created by the chorus'. He goes on to say that whatever motif is central in these plays 'is kept before our minds by the enveloping chorus'.[26] One may imagine a certain tongue in cheek involved in Keane's juxtaposing corner boys and their part in effecting a small town ethos, with the warrior values of Agamemnon. Nevertheless, Kavanagh's encounter with Homer should be borne in mind. When he doubted the significance of the disputed double ditch of rocky ground, the ancient Greek told him that 'I made the *Iliad* from such a *local row*' and that 'Gods make their own importance'.[27]

Whether Keane would have acknowledged corner boys' potential as the stuff of legend is a moot point but he would have agreed that unproductiveness was the single abiding, unarguable aspect of their existence. Idleness has a universal fascination arising from a sense of loss articulated by the story of the Garden of Eden. Cicero's *otium cum dignitate*, nowadays perceived as leisure with dignity, a benison to be aspired to by those in retirement of one kind or another, would appear to be a classical response to the subliminal unease that suggests humankind is wasting life in being unnecessarily productive. But, it hardly refers to the corner boys who were unlikely to get involved in pursuits of any kind; the disapproval they were almost universally subject to disqualified them automatically. Further, one Latin scholar translates the phrase as 'Tranquillity of worthy standing', meaning a leisure acquired by good men who are lauded for their services to the state – their opponents were known as 'desperadoes', a term surely more apt for the corner boys.[28]

Still it is not difficult to uncover considerable questioning of the received wisdom that work is an essential contribution to the dignity of existence. Bertrand Russell asserted 'that a great deal of harm is being done in the modern world by belief in the virtuousness of work, and that the road to happiness and prosperity lies in an organised diminution of work'. In his 'In Praise of Idleness' written in 1932, he makes a substantial claim that would have supported the corner boys:

> It will be said that, while a little leisure is pleasant, men would not know how to fill their days if they had only four hours of work out of the twenty-four. In so far as this is true in the modern world, it is a condemnation of our civilisation; it would not have been true at any earlier period. *There was formerly a capacity for lightheartedness and play which has been to some extent inhibited by the cult of efficiency.* The modern man thinks that everything ought to be done for the sake of something else, and never for its own sake.[29]

Diogenes, the barrel occupying philosopher, provides a more radical support of this paean to the otiose, by attacking the frenetic activity of those who readily believe doing something is better than literally doing nothing:

> When Corinth was threatened with a siege by Philip and all the inhabitants were busily active – one polishing his weapons, another collecting stones, a third repairing the wall – and Diogenes saw

all this, he hurriedly belted his cloak and eagerly trundled his tub up and down the streets. When asked why he was doing that, he answered: I, too, am at work and roll my tub so that I will not be the one and only loafer among so many busy people … [30]

Finally, there is what is probably the most universally approved of leisurely existences and that is the monastic one. There are too many aspects of the corner boys' lifestyle that paralleled the cloister to pass without comment. Corner boys were almost entirely celibate, although involuntarily so – no woman would have them; men being expected to be providers in those days, these were obviously incapable of this and would not have been regarded as potential mates. (This is where a comparison with drones in a bee hive falls down; drones although incapable of defending or taking care of themselves – they are stingless – do perform a function of fertilisation, although the unfortunates are disposed of immediately afterwards). They were poverty stricken and they pursued a life of reflection and contemplation in the sense that they did not engage in any productive or meaningful activity – the biblical reference to considering the 'lilies of the field, [who] neither reap nor sow' is particularly apt. Their seeming indifference to status, which could be inferred from the fact that their behaviour was openly on display on the corners could be argued to be a form of humility. Their lot was a voluntary occupation of a public place where, in full and constant view, they lazed about and idled. In fact their humility could be argued to be even more profound because a life, espousing or embracing the same principles in a monastery, would at least have earned them the respect of the community.

Generally it is acknowledged, and favourably, that the contemplative is pursuing a life devoted to developing a relationship with, or comprehension of, the Supreme Being; there are others who would maintain that the whole motivation is a love of God. The corner boy, who might be described as a secular monk, could be perceived to have

CORNER BOYS IN SMALL TOWN IRELAND, 1922–1970

been under less of an illusion. He probably would acknowledge, fairly readily, his antipathy towards manual labour or indeed any other form of what is conventionally regarded as work. He was pursuing the life of the passive; the audience type rather than the actor. Interestingly, Giles Constable writes that secular monks are mentioned in a twelfth-century text called *A Little Book Concerning the Various Orders and Professions in the Church;* they are described as persons 'whose profession is nothing'.[31] Whatever practises these people may have had, their twentieth-century successors, the corner boys, were just as poor, chaste, humble and even maybe honest as their monastic brethren, past or present, but in a form that subverted the conventional criteria of sanctity and holiness.

Their Purpose in the Community

The distinct probability is that most corner boys were totally unconscious of any *raison d'etre* for how they passed their time, but several observations might be drawn. The term 'corner boy' although originally Irish and in use for one hundred and fifty years, had come to be more specifically relevant to Ireland for about fifty years post independence. In that way, it refers to some aspect of the *zeitgeist* of those times. Although corner boys probably existed all over the world, particularly in economically distressed times, they had a particular resonance in Ireland during the middle decades of the twentieth century. Possibly, the most salient feature of Ireland in those days was its particularly repressed society. In this ethos there appeared to be a requirement in general discourse for a short hand, (the aforementioned antonomasia) for shirker with a penchant for idling. Forming part of a bygone era of over forty years and more, when even the actual actors of those roles would have reached advanced middle age now, it is unlikely that any indisputable answer could be arrived at. Probably the closest that one could come to any kind of satisfactory suggestion is by approaching it laterally. Gayatri Spivak prompts the question – 'Can the corner boy speak'?[32] Is he simply an academic construct? Or is he what Foucault might call an effect of discursive formation, but of what discourse is he a product?

John B. Keane, chronicler of the small town, confirms its common usage in his writings, demonstrating the idea that corner boy is more than likely a result of popular discourse. This has to indicate that the corner boy performed some role, at least in the mind's eye of the user. That purpose was not necessarily a service to the community (an early neighbourhood watch scheme, maybe), or a fulfilling of some need to society (a scapegoat would be one example). It could also have filled some lexical lack – the previously mentioned 'conny dodger' is one, not very perfect example. But it is suggested that the answer, if there be one at all, might lie at a deeper level. Foucault in *Discipline and Punish* believes the arrival of Bentham's Panopticon was 'an event in the "history of the human mind"'. He wrote: 'In appearance, it is merely the solution of a technical problem; but, through it, a whole type of society emerges'.[33] The panopticon was originally a new form of prison where a raised central tower was surrounded by a circle of cells completely open and observable to the authorities in the tower. As a result of its structure, the prisoners were subject to 'permanent, exhaustive, omnipresent surveillance ... like a faceless gaze that transformed the whole social body into a field of perception'.[34] Foucault saw a transition from coercive discipline to the subtler one of continual observation developing. This arose from an idea that discipline by the state and its functionaries was limited and all that could originally be expected of them was 'to neutralise dangers, to fix useless or disturbed populations'. Now, however, with the services of the surveillance mechanics of the panopticon, these institutions were changing and 'were being asked to play a positive role ... to increase the possible utility of individuals'.[35] That is, in other words, if the state could keep a constant eye on its miscreants it could discipline them and turn them into better people, or more correctly, as Foucault would have it, more useful people. This arose from the 'sovereign gaze' whose authority commanded obeisance, or at least compliance of some degree to the decree of the authorities.

Foucault maintained that there then occurred, 'a swarming of disciplinary mechanisms' and these resulted in an inordinate intrusion into the lives of the population in general. He cites, as an example, directives given to charity workers in Paris:

> They will strive to eradicate places of ill-repute, tobacco shops, life classes, gaming houses, public scandals, blasphemy, impiety, and any other disorders that may come to their knowledge ... [They will have to investigate] the stability of the lodging, knowledge of prayers, attendance at the sacraments, knowledge of a trade, morality ... whether they do not allow licentiousness and cajolery in their families, especially in their older daughters.[36]

Thus the whole process of state authoritarianism burgeons inexorably into madness. Acton's dictum of power tending to corrupt is exemplified by the breakdown of compos mentis rather than the more conventional interpretation of corruption as a 'brown envelope' syndrome.

Similarly in Ireland, after 1922, and as referred to at the beginning of this essay, a process of conservatism led to a type of Catholic nationalism that had an undue influence for over fifty years. It must be borne in mind that this was a fledgling arrival, traumatised not just by colonialism but by civil war. Within a few years the country found itself at the mercy of a worldwide depression and an economic war with its main market, England. It is not surprising that a general air of instability permeated the country and led to a ready belief that more rigid controls of governance were required. This coupled with a populace that still, post-colonially, perceived authority as something to be opposed regardless of the seeming benignity of its intentions, prescribed for as much control as possible and additionally for as much assistance in the exercise as possible.

This is where the corner boys' most relevant role emerges. These groups which could be found on the strategic corners of every small town (and city suburb) of Ireland projected the 'sovereign gaze' that Foucault writes about. Lacan's scopic drive, the authority of the gaze, that is the gaze of the tourist, of the colonist, for example and affects the behaviour of the object of this exercise. It inhibits and controls, it is part of the peer pressure that keeps the members of a community abiding by whatever standards of behaviour exist.

Looking at the photograph on the cover of this volume, the three men at the corner (one partially hidden) are peering at the young couple chatting at the other corner. Behind all of them, there are other figures going about their daily tasks. The young couple appear to be oblivious to the attention they are attracting. A close examination of the faces of at least two of these men would suggest that it would be a very difficult thing to ignore them. Although there is no malice in the stares, it is suggested there is little of the affectionate or tolerant regard that would normally be granted young lovers. It operates exactly as Bentham's panopticon, but for one considerable difference.[37] That is, the observed is aware that he is being observed. Now Bentham went to considerable pains in his designs to ensure that the observed could not establish whether he was being subject to surveillance at any particular time. He believed that this accentuated the power of the 'gaze'. In the case of the corner boy, the observed not alone knew whether he was being observed or not, but also knew the identity of the observer. This, I propose, was as cogent, if not more so, than any panopticon. The observer, in a small town, knew the seed and breed, the peccadilloes and the pretensions of the observed. The corner boy was a sentinel, a guardian, maintainer of the morals and mores of the community and as such was an (almost definitely unconscious) buttress to the authorities in their control of the populace.

That the authorities would allow, or even enlist, such reprobates, in the running of the state is a question that could be legitimately asked. In fact the point could be further made that respectable members of the community and those in authority would be horrified at the idea of being somehow in alliance with corner boys. However, if corner boys were not in some way contributing to the community surely they would have been moved on or dispersed. They were generally looked at askance by anyone aspiring to some status and could not have been anything but a source of irritation to those who had to run the gauntlet past them on a regular basis. The authorities, in those days, would have regarded people's rights as a particularly nebulous concept and would have no compunction about getting rid of them. In any case there were regulations about 'unlawful assemblies' that could have been utilised. Corner boys are a classic example of the 'polymorphous techniques of power' which Foucault explains 'is tolerable only on condition that it masks a substantial part of itself. Its success is proportional to its ability to hide its own mechanisms'.[38] In other words, the clandestine operation of authority is when the state is at its most effective in exercising control.

Of course, it would be risible to maintain that there was a conspiracy to enlist these corner boys and submit the communities in small centres of population to their controlling observation. At the very most, there was a tacit acceptance of them, a tolerance of their behaviour, and even this suggests that they were in some way co-operating in 'The Order of Things'. Clearly, the authorities themselves were not conscious of this in any way. On the other hand, comparisons with heroes of that epoch are not entirely surreal. James Bond, who originated in the early 1950s, although portrayed as anarchic in both demeanour and action, was the staunchest defender of the two greatest imperial powers of the twentieth century (albeit at different times). In a different but parallel way, the 'corner boys', despised by the authorities, looked down on by all 'respectable' members of society but admired secretly or otherwise, by quite a few adults and most schoolchildren, were, paradoxically, significant upholders of a community that was too conservative for its own good. They formed part of the fabric of the society in Ireland for fifty years and as such contributed to the mores of those times, serving to control while simultaneously appearing as a mildly subversive symbol of resistance to that same authority.

'Corner boys' became part of popular discourse in Ireland from 1920 to 1970. The people it referred to were probably to be found in every part of the world so the question that arises is what particular resonance did it have in Ireland that the phrase should have found such continual usage? An examination of what corner boys may have represented, what they were perceived as, or indeed what they may have professed throws little light on the question. But when their position is assessed as observers, and subsequently monitors, a valid answer arises. It is suggested here that they formed part of the early surveillance of the state, maybe even a harbinger of the now ubiquitous CCTV. Yet unlike these modern instruments of state control with their implicit threat of nemesis, the corner boy was a far more subtle deterrent, utilising that most cogent regulator of one's actions –'what would the neighbours think?' The paradox is that such perceived reprobates, outsiders, ne'er do wells, should form such a significant cog in the machinery of state power.

6 RETHINKING RURAL/URBAN: TRADITIONAL MUSIC AND MUSICAL COMMUNITY IN 21ST-CENTURY DUBLIN

LAUREN WEINTRAUB STOEBEL

A few years ago, two young Dublin-born traditional musicians released an album to much acclaim. Entitled 'Dublin Made Me,' the CD features duets played by Liam O'Connor on fiddle and Sean McKeon on uilleann pipes, both musicians raised in prominent musical families hailing from the capital city. In a radio interview promoting the CD's release, Liam O'Connor mentioned that while his flute-playing father Mick was born in Dublin's Liberties, his mother actually came from Clare, and the family would frequently spend much of the summer there after attending the Willie Clancy Summer School each year. One summer, a friend introduced Liam at a session as 'a young fiddle player from Dublin … but his mother is from Clare!' The implication was that Liam must have received his music from the side of his family based in a county now thought of as one of the 'heartlands' of traditional music, when in fact the fiddle player inherited much of his music and inspiration from his Dublin-born father.

I begin this essay with this story because I believe that it illustrates one of the ways that popularly-reinforced images of traditional music as indelibly tied to the geography and communal relationships of an idealised rural west of Ireland do not adequately represent the complex experiences of many musicians engaging with music today. Rather than rehash tales of urban musical experience framed exclusively in relation to rural Ireland, this essay instead examines the everyday creation and dissolution of musical life in present-day Dublin in its own right. By highlighting the fluid roles of prominent institutions and the creative use of urban spaces, I will explore not only the unique musical geography of the city, but the connections and flows between Dublin's musical communities and others throughout Ireland. The integration of musical expression within the everyday lives of Dublin residents will be integral to this understanding, and will be featured via ethnographic methodologies, participant observation and interviews.

Like Liam O'Connor's story above, popular representations of Irish traditional music very much capitalise on its roots in certain parts of the west of Ireland. When scholars and the popular media conceptualise the role of the urban musician in Ireland, they most frequently tell versions of two different stories. The first story is that of the urban, usually middle-class revivalist's role in preserving and popularising traditional music in the 1950s and 1960s in Ireland. The iconic figure of composer Seán Ó Riada, for example, stands alongside later commercial performing groups such as Planxty and the Bothy Band and radio pioneers such as Ciarán Mac Mathúna and Seamus Ennis in popularising traditional music amongst new audiences. The second frequently heard story is of the city-based musician who was either born in the country or who rediscovers family roots there, and who identifies almost exclusively with that rural 'homeland'. (This is the story imposed on Liam O'Connor in the anecdote at the beginning of this paper.) In versions of this story, rural musicians often don't feel musically or socially 'at home' in urban environments[1] or they make frequent trips – sometimes even characterised as 'pilgrimages' – to rural areas or to festivals held in the west.[2] While aspects of both of these common stories are certainly true, in reality they are complicated by contradictions – from families such as the O'Connors and McKeons who have now been rooted in Dublin for multiple generations, to rural, middle-class newcomers to traditional music who come to the music later in life but who still become respected musical figures in their communities.

Conceptualising Music, Place and Community

Some recent scholarship on Irish traditional music has begun to provide alternatives to these popular narratives about the role of place, space and geography in the history of Irish traditional music. These approaches include re-evaluations of the concept of 'regional style', or the role of islands, towns, and cities in narratives surrounding traditional music.[3] For example, Fintan Vallely and Gary Hastings have both written about traditional music in Northern Ireland, examining the complex ways that musical performance intersects with sectarian identities, often not conforming to preconceived notions regarding politically-bounded communities.[4] Vallely, in particular, explores the ways that the common perception of 'traditional music as Catholic music' neglects a complex history in which Protestant individuals and communities have shared in the performance of tunes and songs now considered to be the core repertoire of Irish traditional music. More broadly, authors such as Helen O'Shea have begun to challenge the common description of a traditional music pub 'session' experience in which musicians come together to play music that transcends social, cultural or economic distinctions. This approach aims to deconstruct stereotypical notions of 'community', common to both ethnomusicology and Irish Studies, in which community elides individual perspectives on group musical performance, focusing instead on an 'embodied, transcendent experience of an ideal society' rather than the more difficult aspects of change, ambiguity and difference.[5] O'Shea's goals echo those of Richard Kearney, who calls for a postmodern republic in Ireland in which a 'community' means a place where 'identity is part of a permanent process of narrative retelling, where each citizen is in a state of dependency on others'. In such a postmodern republic, the principle of interdependency is seen as a virtue rather than a vice; it serves, in fact, as a reminder that every citizen's story is related to every other's'.[6]

These types of projects attempting to confront change and difference in the context of ideas about communities have also been at the core of recent anthropological and ethnomusicological projects attempting to reconcile local urban musical practices with processes of globalisation or migration. In 1982, Adelaida Reyes-Schramm, one of the first ethnomusicologists to theorise music-related research in an urban environment, placed an emphasis on concepts of diversity and difference in her approach to an 'urban ethnomusicology'.[7] She writes of how most city residents have access to 'diverse musical resources and are conversant with multiple sets of socio-musical rules'. They are thus able to 'invoke a particular set [of rules] that is appropriate to each of the many contexts that are part of urban existence'.[8] This emphasis on choosing between diverse cultural or musical resources remains a common theme in the ethnomusicological and anthropological study of cities,[9] but it is a theme that is increasingly complicated by the spread of technologies and the movement of people back and forth between cities and other environments.

Indeed, the 'problem' of a diverse urban environment has preoccupied other ethnographers as well, many of whom have struggled to find an alternative to older, more rigidly bounded definitions of 'community'. In an attempt to gain a holistic view of musical activity in a mid-sized English town, Ruth Finnegan writes of how more commonly-used terms such as network, group, association, world, community or scene did not quite capture the ways that people related to each other in the town through musical practices.[10] Echoing Reyes-Schramm's emphasis on diversity, Finnegan instead settles on an idea of 'pathways' as a metaphor for music-based relationships in the town of Milton Keynes:

> Far from being the kind of marginal and unstructured activity often suggested by the label 'leisure', with its implications of residual items somehow left over from 'real' life, ['the residents'] musical practices were upheld not by isolated individuals in an asocial vacuum or by people merely trying to fill the time to 'solve' the 'problem of leisure', but through a series of socially recognised pathways which systematically linked into a wide variety of settings and institutions within the city.[11]

While the motivations for these scholars attempting to lay new lexical ground for ethnography in urban areas are understandable, this essay maintains the concept of community as the grounding ethos for its analysis. This is partly because of the many ways in which community now commonly refers to relationships beyond the 'traditional' community bound by discrete (typically rural) geographical or political boundaries, including communities linked through travel and technologies. The concept of community already pervades the discourse surrounding Irish traditional music on many levels. Community is used in reference to music's role in Irish national culture – an intangible sense of national culture and unity, along the lines of Anderson's 'imagined community'.[12] This can emerge in mild patriotic terms as well as more strident political ones, such as the role of musical performances in conflict and reconciliation between the Catholic and Protestant communities in Northern Ireland. Community is also used in reference to processes of globalisation – a shifting and growing global 'trad community' referenced in counterpoint to the music's perceived roots in locally-based performance. And community is especially prominent in cultural policy discussions about traditional music, from 'community development' to 'community arts'. My choice to use community as an identifier is specifically because the redefinition applies to more than just urban environments. It is not only helpful to incorporate diversity and difference into a conception of community in order to better apply it to urban situations, but in doing so it also expands the range of 'normal' or 'authentic' group relationships across Ireland – between the North and the Republic; among farmland, town and city; among upper, middle and lower classes; among citizens and immigrants or tourists; and among men, women and children.

Placing Traditional Music in Dublin

Of course, no matter how much more intensively technology, travel and migration globally connect a city such as Dublin, it is also still shaped by its own particular histories and geographies, which relate to musical performance and community. Dublin's most obvious geographical feature is the river Liffey, which divides the city's centre into two halves. The northern and southern halves of the city, however, are also loosely stereotyped by affiliations of class and politics, with many parts of the northside often identified as working-class or populist, and large swaths of the southside identified as middle- or upper-class or Anglo-Irish. Over the past fifty years or more, suburban neighbourhoods have also spiralled outwards from the more concentrated city centre, each with more or less a discrete identity. These outer neighbourhoods or suburbs, sometimes incorporating formerly rural towns, centre on identifying features from shopping centres to schools to more typical 'town centres' featuring restaurants, shops and pubs.

The expansion of Dublin's city boundaries in the second half of the twentieth century coincided with larger demographic change throughout Ireland, as the country's majority population shifted from being rural to urban. The migrant workers and new residents in the city also included many musicians from other regions of the country. This influx of new musical life at a time when traditional music throughout the country was suffering from a lack of respect and interest not only helped to revive older Dublin-based institutions such as the Dublin Pipers' Club, but would later contribute to the founding of Comhaltas Ceoltóirí Éireann (commonly translated as the Association of Irish Musicians), Na Píobairí Uilleann (the Pipers' Club), numerous professional performing groups and other highly visible symbols of musical revival. Certain city neighbourhoods also waxed and waned through these mid-century decades as traditional music hubs, either through the graces of a generous publican who hosted music, or, in areas like the 'Liberties' through a critical mass of musicians living there at various times.

As mentioned, the stories of traditional music in Dublin most frequently told are, perhaps justifiably, those of these important musicians – often migrating from elsewhere in Ireland – who galvanised instrumental performance in the city from the 1950s and 1960s. The pub and house sessions of those decades, along with the folk clubs and professional bands of the 1960s and 1970s, have long defined the image of urban traditional music performance in Ireland. In spite of the lasting impact of these exceptional examples, however, they no longer encapsulate the everyday contemporary pathways of musical experience in Dublin and its environs. Building upon this important history, the following two examples from the musical life (and geography) of contemporary Dublin explore how notions of musical community are cultivated and coveted in the twenty-first century Irish city, particularly the importance of musical spaces in creating community and the symbolic role of clubs and associations.

The focus in these examples is on performances that to some extent depend on 'participatory' musical expression – 'process-oriented' performance in which most of those present are actively involved in the musical experience to some degree.[13] While it is often hard to completely separate these types of performances from a continuum that leads to more commercial events with a typical performer/audience relationship, notions of musical community often depend on the existence of these participatory musical expressions. And, in turn, it is these participatory performances that continue to allow traditional music to interweave itself through the everyday lives of Irish communities throughout the island and the world.

Musical Spaces in Dublin: The Cobblestone

The flows and points of contact shaping traditional music and musical community in Dublin cannot be considered without addressing the physical spaces in which these processes occur. In fact, the built spaces of the city stand at the nexus of distinctions between the categories of urban and rural, as elucidated by geographer Andrew MacLaran, 'One useful way of viewing the urban environment is to regard it as marking a transformation in the use to which land is put, rural environments being characterised by land-extensive operations, while urban functions are largely land-intensive. Of course, within these two broad categories there are considerable degrees of variation in intensiveness, but it is a useful distinction because it focuses upon the very essence of 'the urban: the way in which land is used and the character of the built environment'.[14]

While traditional music flourishes in numerous spaces throughout the city, from front parlours to street corners to union halls to concert stages, this analysis will focus on one of the most dynamic of these spaces: the pub. The pub has been an essential site in the performance and transmission of traditional music in Ireland since the 1960s, but I will be focusing on the role of one particular Dublin pub in the context of traditional music performance, The Cobblestone.[15]

The Cobblestone can be geographically situated in a number of different ways. Perhaps most obviously, it serves as the 'local' in the neighbourhood of Smithfield, which is located at the western extreme of the city centre's 'Northside'. The Smithfield neighbourhood is centred around a large, open, paved market square which was extensively rehabilitated starting in 1997. A recent *New York Times* travel article[16] promoted Smithfield as exemplifying successful development in Dublin, highlighting the bright and glistening new hotel, supermarket and cinema. The weekly multicultural market is the perfect symbol of the diverse residents of the new apartment blocks lining the square who mix in with the working-class homes and residents still left in the area.

But for every new business around the square, there are also signs of the limits of urban re-development plans – shuttered shops and hotels, as well as prime real estate in newly-constructed buildings which have never been occupied by any tenants. In fact, in addition to the Cobblestone itself, the top of the square is dominated by the shells of empty, half-demolished buildings. As the pub's prominent place in the *New York Times* article shows, however, the Cobblestone clearly also serves other populations besides Smithfield locals. Via word of mouth, music session listings on the web and tourist guidebooks – among other sources – the pub is also known throughout Ireland and globally as a music-friendly space. The prominence of traditional music is actually a relatively new development for this pub, which has been a pub since at least the nineteenth century, but only became the Cobblestone and a 'music pub' as recently as the early 1990s. Current owner Tom Mulligan hails from a music-friendly family and the Cobblestone's reputation for both traditional music and other types of concerts helps ensure that it is packed nearly every night of the week. Even the geography within the pub suggests the importance of musicians to the pub's atmosphere and bottom line – a small area at the front is reserved 'for musicians only' by way of a small sign. Pictures of musicians and advertisements for concerts plaster nearly every wall, and the back room is used nearly exclusively for concerts, with valuable floor space taken up by a stage and a sound system.

Thus, through its local and international reputation, the Cobblestone connects many different intersecting webs of people. It serves as a quirky and comfortable watering hole for locals from the neighbourhood. Traditional musicians from around the city and suburbs travel considerable distances to play at daily (or sometimes twice-daily) pub sessions. Music-friendly audiences of all types come for frequent concerts of various genres held in the back room. Dancers assemble for weekly set dancing classes and monthly céilís with live music. Learning musicians meet weekly in the back room for a 'slow' or 'learners' session away from the eyes of an audience.

For all of these individuals, the space of the pub acts as a nexus between public and private musical experiences. Commercial enterprise, tourism and concert performance intersect neatly with family legacies, safe space for learning and transmission, and 'participatory' music and dance. In this sense the Cobblestone combines a cosmopolitan sensibility common to cities[17] with musical expressions that are more rooted in participants' local and national identities. In fact, in terms of the built space of the pub and its environs, it could very well be the lacklustre performance of the Smithfield development project that fosters a casual, multi-use space such as the Cobblestone, versus the successful and highly managed development of the Temple Bar area. The organic overlapping of different communities within the space of the pub stands in contrast to the Temple Bar development project as described by Gerry Smyth: 'The [Temple Bar] project is also susceptible to the criticism that it attempts to manufacture in a controlled environment an impression of random organic space, whereas in fact such spaces emerge, as Michel de Certeau explained with recourse to a linguistic metaphor, only as an ambiguous, vernacular response to the urban grammar constructed by planners and architects – a second, poetic geography on top of the geography of the literal, forbidden or permitted meaning.'[18] The organic space of the pub – fostered by the management – allows both the translocal experience of the musical tourist or the popular music performer to overlap with the specifically Dublin-based musical relationships of long-time set dance partners or traditional session compatriots; neither mode of musical experience subsumes or negates the other.

Musical Associations and Clubs: Comhaltas Ceoltóirí Éireann

While a pub serves as a physical space that can cultivate or solidify communities via musical performance, there are also many different types of clubs and associations around the city that act as symbolic umbrellas under which communities grow and change. Historically, these types of groups have served an important role in the development of Dublin's musical communities, both in their own right and building on and fostering relationships connected to the physical spaces discussed above – from neighbourhoods to pubs and union or political halls. While one of the oldest examples is the Dublin Pipers' Club (founded in 1900),[19] some of the strongest associations emerged in the mid-twentieth century as the aforementioned migration of musicians into the city created a strong demand for new physical and symbolic spaces for participatory musical expression. Piper and activist Gay McKeon speaks fondly of the early years of the Thomas Street Pipers' Club, for example, in which musicians and musical aficionados such as his parents found a sympathetic community, based around shared experiences of migration as well as shared political and cultural affinities:

> A social event for my parents was going to the Pipers' Club, and committee meetings … And I was only reflecting on it recently that there was a real sense of community, there. It was really strong. And a huge emphasis on young people … It was very much a sense of identity. And it felt, very – I wouldn't necessarily say republican, but Irish heritage and culture. But it was mainly run by country men and women, who came to live in Dublin.[20]

Clubs for traditional Irish music such as the Thomas Street and Church Street gatherings proved to be important umbrellas under which participants could negotiate their own relationships to rural origins and urban realities. The question of identification with both rural and urban homes is a complicated one. For example, a 1962 RTÉ field recording from the Church Street Club features an interview with tinwhistle player Pat White who makes a point of the fact that he is not from Dublin, but from Mullagh (in Co. Clare, located in the south-west of Ireland), in spite of the fact that he's lived in Dublin for thirty-one years.[21] These clubs also played a role in the shifting perception of traditional music outside of the club's 'safe space' in the public sphere of mid-twentieth-century Ireland. A common trope recurs frequently in descriptions of musical life, both urban and rural, at this time: the fiddle player who must hide his instrument under his coat as he travels to and from home in order to avoid being 'outed' as a musician. The 'activist' cultural projects referenced by McKeon in the above quote stood in strong contrast to these negative tropes.

In today's Dublin, these types of groups include school- and university-based clubs, Gaelic Athletic Association clubs, unions, Na Píobairí Uilleann and, representing the largest number of members of a single organisation dedicated to traditional music, branches of Comhaltas Ceoltóirí Éireann. This analysis will focus primarily on the multifaceted role of Comhaltas in Dublin.

Comhaltas was founded in 1951 with the aim of promoting and preserving Irish traditional music and dance, starting with the founding of a national festival and competition, Fleadh Cheoil na hÉireann. Over the ensuing decades, however, the organisation grew from an annual event to a network of hundreds of branches throughout Ireland and the world. This expansion included many branches in cities, though Comhaltas consistently maintains a revivalist orientation, frequently identifying traditional music with the Irish countryside.

While the most public and perhaps most controversial face of Comhaltas is its role as a national and international organisation, many, if not most, members think of themselves first and foremost as members of their local branch. The national organisation runs larger-scale programming such as teacher training programmes, traditional music exams, concerts and tours, but it is the local branches that determine the needs of the communities they serve and organise everything from music lessons, to preparation for competitions, to concerts, sessions and céilí dances.

The greater Dublin area is served by upwards of ten branches of various sizes, each based in a specific neighbourhood either just outside the city centre or a little bit further out in a more suburban community. Branches usually do not have their own facility dedicated to music, so activities such as music lessons, group rehearsals and sessions often share spaces such as GAA clubhouses, local schools and multi-purpose community centres. But while a neighbourhood such as Beaumont, Clontarf or Ballinteer may serve as the nucleus for the branch, the largest branches draw members from around the city for a variety of reasons and from a variety of backgrounds. For members, the branch serves in a couple of capacities. On the one hand it can solidify or make explicit other 'pathways' or connections, such as family relationships, neighbourhood connections, school friendships or relationships developed via spaces such as pubs or other clubs. On the other hand, a club or association can also act as a gateway for those who are not yet part of an existing musical community, taking the place of other motivations for becoming involved in participatory music such as the influence of other musicians in the family. My own research on Comhaltas throughout Ireland has shown these motivations to be relatively consistent in branches throughout the island, from rural to urban and in-between.

The agendas of members include personal self-expression, family allegiance, and opportunities for socialisation — all interspersed with the politics of cultural identity. For both students and parents, one of the key benefits of belonging to a branch is the face-to-face interaction that is essential to the transmission and enjoyment of traditional music. Students consistently remark that they make close and lasting friendships both with their fellow musicians in the local branch, as well as with the other musicians they meet across the country at various competitions and festivals in the summertime. Parents and other family members become involved as well, filling the heavy demand for volunteer leadership within the branch, as well as participating in group holiday trips and other events.

Many of the current Comhaltas student members were, unlike some of their parents, born and raised in Dublin and feel a strong identification with music in the city. These students are well aware of both the current strength of traditional music in Dublin and the city's unique position as an iconic location for traditional music that does not fit into the rubric of a rural region with a distinct musical 'style' or accent. In an interview with Northside community radio station NearFM, Beaumont Comhaltas teacher Aoife O'Brien says that she believes that traditional music in Dublin today is:

> … definitely strong. I don't see how anybody could say that it's weakening in any way. It's definitely going from strength to strength. And … we're so lucky in Dublin to have people coming to work in the city from the four different corners of the country, you get all the different styles kinda mixed into one, which makes it really interesting.[22]

As important as Comhaltas has been in cultivating new spaces for transmission and performance in certain areas of the city, the relationship between the local branch and the national organisation can sometimes be at odds, and branches in the urban environment also face unique challenges. A recent widely-publicised struggle between the Clontarf branch and the Comhaltas headquarters over control of a gleaming new purpose-built traditional music centre just north-east of the city centre illustrates how the priorities and personalities at the centre of a local community can come into conflict with the leadership of a less concrete 'imagined' national community.

And while an urban location and the resources and influence that emerge from physical proximity to government funding and power can be of great benefit to a Dublin Comhaltas branch, urban branches are also fighting with numerous other interests for a practical and symbolic role for traditional music in the public spaces of the city. For example, in Munster or Connacht, the annual provincial fleadh or competition can literally take over the town which hosts it – closing down streets, hosting outdoor concerts that can be heard through nearly the whole town, prompting pubs and restaurants to host music which normally would have little to do with a session. By way of contrast, the 2008 Leinster fleadh was held in the Dublin suburb of Dundrum, and while sessions were held and local schools were taken over with competitions, the colonisation of local public space mostly extended to a few square metres of the plaza in the middle of Dundrum shopping centre.

Conclusion

Examining the above case studies can lead us towards a flexible definition of musical community and its relationship to place, geography and concepts of 'the ordinary', that applies beyond the urban environment. Firstly, community is plural, involving different intersecting communities and no community exists outside of its relationship to other groups. In the study of music, this idea is a revision of a common earlier focus within musical study on performance demarcating a singular 'folk group'. The Cobblestone, for example, provides a single environment in which different communities intersect productively for all involved. Secondly, community does not deny the individual. In particular, in the context of formalised communities such as Comhaltas Ceoltóirí Éireann, this requires an anthropological emphasis on the importance of analysing both the discourse and actions of the State and other organisations in the public sphere, as well as the decisions and interactions of the individuals constituting these structures of power.[23] The ethnographer is charged with challenging face-value interpretations of organisational or governmental discourse and determining whether individual intentions align with either actions or eventual outcomes in the context of group power.[24] An individual belonging to a group or a community, formally or informally, might express opinions counter to the ideology of that group, and those opinions might again contradict the individual's actions or the outcomes arising from those actions. And finally, community is a process that is constantly shifting and changing through time and across space. In this context, it is also performed and constructed through time by the actions of individuals.[25] Using this concept, Gregory Barz writes of the Tanzanian *kwaya* as a community of *performance* that 'typically functions as a direct connection between one's cultural past and present. In this way community is not a static object; rather it is a process by which people come together for a particular cause or purpose'.[26] Combining these three core concepts, then, examining traditional music in the urban context of Dublin leads us to a working definition of 'community' that is loosely adapted from the work of Michael Herzfeld on the concept of cultural intimacy[27]: musical community is performances of collective selfhood.

Both the Cobblestone and the Comhaltas branches give musicians and others a sense of connection – a sense of place and community that is connected to the geography of the city but not bounded by it. In other words, these musical communities facilitate the performance and development of collective selfhood. This is, perhaps, what geographer Doreen Massey refers to as 'progressive' or 'global' sense of place, 'the product of layer upon layer of different sets of linkages, both local and to the wider world'.[28] This kind of amorphous and flexible relationship between music, people and place – rural, urban or otherwise – is summed up eloquently by Paddy Glackin who, when asked to describe what being a 'Dublin musician' means, responded thus:

> Ok, it's very simple. It's to do with your environment. It's to do with the people you've met. It's to do with association. It's all very, very personal stuff. It's to do with people you've grown up with. It's to do with their accents. It's to do with the sounds that they make. It's

to do with the physical environment. It's all of that which makes a
Dublin musician. It's to do with our sense of humour. Which would
be quite different to people of the country … And there's a feeling
I have that I find very difficult to put a word on. But it's a kind of
a comfort … and all the architecture of Dublin and all the sounds
of Dublin are compatible, as far as I'm concerned. So it's not just
about – I'm not wearing a badge. I'm not wearing a football jersey.
I'm not wearing a colour here. It's a very deeply personal thing.
That's what being a Dublin musician means to me.[29]

This progressive sense of place allows Dublin musicians to absorb
categories such as rural and urban and then move beyond them to explore
shared ways that people relate to music and the places and communities
in which they live.

7 THE RIDDLE OF RAVENHILL: THE 1954 IRISH RUGBY INTERNATIONAL IN BELFAST

VIC RIGBY AND LIAM O'CALLAGHAN

In 2006, the Irish rugby team played its first home match in Belfast for over fifty years when Italy visited Ravenhill. In the build-up to the game, some discordant voices were raised by the Irish Rugby Football Union's decision not to allow *God Save Our Queen* to be played before the match. It was customary for *The Soldier's Song* to be played at equivalent occasions in Dublin and a clutch of unionist politicians thought the same protocol should be extended to an international taking place on British soil. It was a concern brusquely dismissed by the IRFU, with a spokesman touchily asserting that: 'Symbols and emblems should be put to one side … This is a game and a sport'.[1]

This reaction was symptomatic of the long-standing Irish Rugby Football Union (IRFU) policy of political neutrality. The IRFU was founded in 1879 and, with jurisdiction over rugby in the thirty-two counties of the island, is a non-partitionist body. In addition, the game can claim, with some legitimacy, to appeal to all traditions on the island. In the south, the sport has traditionally appealed to the broadly nationalist Catholic middle-classes, while in Ulster rugby is solidly Protestant and unionist. The Irish international XV acknowledges this pluralism by playing under a neutral flag and standing to attention to the anodyne *Ireland's Call*, a song that, of necessity, has no political content.[2] With some Protestant players claiming that representing Ireland in rugby allows them to feel a flexible sense of Irishness,[3] the game has achieved a level of ostensible solidarity that other major sports in Ireland such as Gaelic games and soccer cannot lay claim to.

This solidarity was almost fatally compromised in 1954 by an incident that is the focus of this study and highlights the difficulty in separating sport from politics in Ireland. In what Sean Diffley has termed 'the most closely-guarded secret in Irish rugby', the ten southern players selected to play against Scotland in Belfast that season almost refused to take the field in protest at having to stand to attention to *God Save Our Queen*. Only the fraught intervention of IRFU officials and the promise that all future internationals would take place south of the border prevented a course of action that could have led to a damaging split in Irish rugby.[4] The IRFU, understandably, was eager to keep the episode as confidential as possible and discretion was strongly encouraged among the players involved. Though Diffley would claim, in recounting the events in 1973, that 'this is the first public reference to the incident',[5] details of the controversy had been in the public domain much earlier. Arguing against a proposal to hold an international match in Belfast in 1963, the *Irish Press* recalled the 1954 incident:

A large number of Southern players on the Irish team on that occasion protested strongly beforehand and said they wouldn't play in the match if the British anthem was played as the anthem for the Irish team. Up to quarter of an hour before the time scheduled for the kick-off the crisis existed … A situation like that should never be allowed again and the best way of avoiding it is to play all home internationals at Lansdowne Road, where our own anthem and flag are duly honoured.[6]

Yet secrecy and *de facto* denial remained the official policy of the rugby authorities. Edmund van Esbeck, in a book officially sanctioned by the IRFU to mark its hundredth anniversary in 1979, does not mention the incident and limits his comments on the match to the mundanity of recording the scoreline and absences through injury. Given his stature as a rugby writer in Ireland, it is not credible that he did not know of the incident and its omission from his volume amounts to self-censorship.[7]

When enquiries were made into the affair fifty years later, the IRFU was reticent to offer any relevant insights.[8] This reluctance extended to individuals involved, with one of the southern players replying to a tentative query by writing: 'The least said the better for both Irish rugby and Northern Ireland politics so, sorry, no comment'.[9] Even so, sufficient information from five other players in the Ireland team that day, along with insights from two other contemporary players provides a clear account of what happened, in the players' own words.

Rugby football and Irish politics

Despite the IRFU's best efforts, the origins of rugby in Ireland and the broader sporting and cultural context in which it developed meant that Irish sport could never completely operate in an apolitical vacuum. The first formal rugby club in Ireland was founded at Trinity College Dublin in 1854. By the 1870s, clubs had sprung up in most urban areas of the island and in 1879 the IRFU was founded and an Irish international rugby team began playing regularly against the other nations of the British Isles.[10] By the turn of the twentieth century rugby had acquired a broader socio-cultural constituency, becoming the game of choice among private Catholic schools (as it had been among Protestant schools) and, in Limerick, among the working classes. However, the game remained, and would remain for several decades, heavily

influenced at administrative level by individuals from the northern and
southern Protestant communities. In this context, the game presented
an easy target for cultural nationalists and was popularly branded a
'foreign sport' in contradistinction to Gaelic games.[11] Moreover, there
was something of a disjuncture south of the border between the game's
largely Protestant and unionist administrative structure and its Catholic
grassroots.[12]

Indeed, it was the internal politics of the game that held the most
potential for controversy, particularly in the area of cultural symbolism.
In keeping with its understandable eagerness to maintain compromise
in the arena of political identity, the IRFU decided from 1925 that a
symbolically neutral flag would be flown in place of the tricolour from
thereon in at international matches. Louis Daly, secretary of the Munster
Branch summed up the rationale for the policy in a letter to the Union's
secretary, Rupert Jeffares, in 1932:

> The IRFU were wise enough in 1925 to foresee that at some future
> date, that there was a likelihood of some controversy as regards
> politics entering into the game and decided to steer clear of it by
> striking the flag embodying their four provinces and since then
> they have adhered to their decision to fly this flag, only, at all
> internationals in Ireland. In my opinion, we are not insulting or
> casting any slur on the tricolour or Union Jack, by not flying either,
> as rugby football in Ireland knows no border.[13]

This policy eventually led to a heated campaign in the press in 1932 for
the re-instatement of the tricolour and when the Free State government
intervened, the IRFU relented. Interestingly, much of the disquiet at
the IRFU's flag policy came from within the game. Clubs such as those
at University College Cork, University College Galway and University
College Dublin and a number of clubs in Munster were particularly
strident in their opposition to what was seen as 'anti-national' sentiment

within the game's governing body.[14] Of these, UCD was the most outspoken. In the midst of the 1932 flag controversy, the club's secretary, F.J. Mangan, complained that 'the continuance of the toast of his Britannic Majesty at IRFU dinners ... is an offence to the vast majority of players of the game in the country'. He concluded that the UCD club had always been 'the guardian of national principles in connection with the administration of Rugby football in Ireland'.[15] There was a clear heterogeneity of political viewpoint, therefore, within Irish rugby.

Flags and symbols informed the immediate context to events in Belfast in 1954. Since the mid-1920s, unionist executives in Northern Ireland had treated nationalist rituals such as the public commemoration of the 1916 Easter Rising and the accompanying display of republican symbols as a threat to the state's constitutional status. Under the auspices of the Special Powers Act 1922, the Royal Ulster Constabulary (RUC) was empowered, from 1933, to prohibit the display of the tricolour even when no prevailing threat to public order existed.[16] In 1954, the Brookeborough administration introduced the Flags and Emblems Act in order to shore up unionist rule in the face of internal restlessness among loyalist ultras. The Act made it an offence for any individual to interfere with the display of the Union flag while also prohibiting the display of symbols that could cause a breach of the peace. In essence, therefore, the Act placed a *de facto* prohibition on the flying of the Republic's tricolour in the six counties. Though its genesis lay within the internal politics of unionism, the Act was justifiably seen as symbolising the sectarian irredentism of the unionist regime.

Of more direct relevance is the fact that trouble had been brewing at rugby internationals in Belfast for a while. On the occasion of the Ireland versus Wales international at Ravenhill in 1950, a University College Dublin (UCD) student, Joe Hughes, ran on to the pitch with the Republic's flag before being roughly handled by the RUC. The *Irish Press* gleefully recorded the incident as follows:

While a district Inspector and two constables grappled with him for possession of the flag, Joe gallantly defended it and triumphantly emerged from the scrum still holding the Tricolour and a great cheer went up from the crowd, Irish and Welsh ... Travelling to Belfast on Saturday members of the Rugby club to which Mr Hughes belongs had their cars searched and any Tricolours which could be found by RUC men were seized.[17]

The *Sunday Independent* reacted as follows:

The incident involving the Irish flag at Ravenhill was most unfortunate ... This unprecedented demonstration in the Northern capital, combined with the record number of Tricolours in evidence around the whole arena was a striking manifestation of the strong national feelings of the vast majority of Irish rugby followers. The "foreign game" obviously does not cramp their patriotism! Welsh visitors to whom I spoke were amazed to know that the national flag of Ireland is banned in the Six Counties though the flag of Soviet Russia not.[18]

This was not the only time the southern flag was unfurled at Ravenhill. Robin Roe, Ireland's hooker in the 1954 Belfast game, recalled: 'Police used to try to seize the tricolour because some of the people from the south would come up to the game and when no-one was looking all of a sudden you saw a tricolour. And of course the North saw this as IRA and republicanism. I can assure you it was a very sensitive area'.[19]

In the season before the 1954 incident, Ireland played France in Ravenhill. The *Connacht Sentinel* reacted angrily to the playing of the British national anthem before the match:

What, one wonders, is to be the attitude of the thousands of decent young Irish Rugby players up and down the country to the IRFU who are responsible for the formalities on the field on the day of an international game in this country. We feel confident that they will not stand in favour of the Belfast incident. Indeed many players in the West are already discussing the form in which they should make a strong protest … Strongly entrenched in the higher administrative offices of the Irish Rugby Football Union is, apparently, a clique which stands for British rule for part of the Northern province of Ireland and which, we feel sure, would like to see the Twenty-six Counties again occupied by Britain. To these people the six British-occupied counties are British territory, their people subjects of the British Crown … Members of the Irish team have been criticised for playing under the circumstances. The fact is that they did play and the only thing to be done is to consider what steps are to be taken to ensure that in future Ireland will not be insulted as it was in Belfast … The overwhelming majority of members of rugby clubs in this country maintain that they are as proud of their Irish nationality as those who play the distinctly Irish games. There are many who will judge them in light of their reaction to the Ravenhill affair. The vigour with which they will make and press a protest will be taken by many as the measure of their claim to be loyal Irishmen … Steps should be taken to ensure that any Irishman uncouth enough to give studied insult to his country should not have a place on the councils of an organisation that describes itself as Irish.[20]

Significantly the writer in question identified the perceived political dissonance between the game's administrative establishment and its grassroots throughout the country.

The Ravenhill Incident

The range of political views that any Ireland XV could possess meant, ultimately, that latent tension potentially lay beneath the surface of an ostensibly united international team. That weekend in Belfast, the Irish team comprised ten southerners and five northerners.[21] As was customary in Belfast internationals, the southern Irish players were expected to acknowledge the Union Jack and stand to attention for the British national anthem, whereas the tricolour would not be flown and the Republic's anthem, *Soldier's Song*, would not be sung.

It was customary at this time for the southern contingent to meet in Dublin, take the Belfast train and meet up with the northerners at the Grand Central Hotel in the northern capital. This was the case when ten southern players, together with IRFU officials, met at Amiens Street Station (now Connolly Station), Dublin on Friday, 26 February 1954 for the two-hour journey north. It was on the train that the first signs of unrest emerged. James McCarthy, the captain that day, recalled:

> On the journey, three of the chaps started, not arguing, but discussing about having to be presented to the Governor General of Northern Ireland and having to stand to attention for the British national anthem. They said we're playing for Ireland – it's all wrong ... So one word led to another, as they sometimes do, in a good-natured way, but things got a bit serious and they said look, we don't think we should go out until after the anthem has been played. So the next morning, the day of the match, there was a knock at my door at the hotel. There were the three and some others along for the ride and they said they were not going to go out on the field for God Save the Queen.[22]

Roe, a southerner and Protestant clergyman, had similar memories about the build-up to the match. He recalled:

We had a certain group whose names I won't give you on the Irish side, Southern Ireland, rabid nationalists. They tried to brainwash all of us … that they wouldn't go out because the national anthem that was played was *God Save the Queen*. The argument was that more than half the team was Southern Ireland and why should they stand for the Queen playing at home.[23]

Winger Maurice Mortell, also on the train north, remembered becoming aware of the problem only on the morning of the match. Mortell, who later scored two tries in the game, recalled:

I was checking my football gear in the bedroom at the Grand Central Hotel when two of my teammates knocked on the door. They explained that a number of the players from the South were unhappy at having *God Save the Queen* played as the "home team" anthem when the Irish national anthem was the *Soldier's Song*. My recollection of my response was that my only worry was how I was going to mark Grant Weatherstone, my opposite number on the Scottish team, and that I couldn't care less if they played the Red Flag. However, I added that if the majority of the Southern Irish players felt strongly enough about the matter that I would go along with the decision. Shortly after this discussion, a meeting was held of the 10 Southern Irish players on the team. After everyone had their say it was clear that the great majority were not in favour of having to stand to attention while the British national anthem was being played as that of the home team. However, we all were aware of the delicacy of the situation and after further discussion we agreed that we would ask the executives of the Irish Rugby Union to delay entry of the players on to the pitch until after the national anthem had been played. I think that Jim McCarthy was given the task of conveying this decision to the then secretary of the IRFU, Billy Jeffares, as he [McCarthy] was captain of the team in the absence of Jack Kyle through injury.[24]

It certainly appears that Mortell, and perhaps all his southern teammates, did not expect any difficulty over missing the anthem and coming out on to the pitch later than customary. He remembered: 'In my innocence, I believed that this was a perfectly reasonable solution to what appeared to me to be a fairly minor problem … We never thought there would be any repercussions. We just thought we would stay off the pitch and get on with the game afterwards'.[25] Mortell and his southern colleagues were soon denuded of any such innocence. Recalling what happened as the bus was about to take the players to a lunch on the way to the match, he said:

> When we were joined by our five Ulster teammates, I don't think any of us felt it necessary to tell them what had taken place. We all boarded the coach together outside the Grand Central Hotel to take us to the ground at around 12 o' clock. We had been sitting there for about five minutes waiting for the alickadoos [rugby parlance for committee men] to arrive when Billy Jeffares emerged from the hotel and asked that all the southern players disembark and return to the hotel. The Ulster players were bewildered but I had a sinking feeling that there was trouble in store.[26]

The southern players were told to return to the hotel because of what McCarthy had told the IRFU committeemen. Roe remembered: 'That caused such a row. There was a terrific fear that rugby would split and that Ulster would break away from the South. There was hell to pay. These people were terrified, these people at the top. They wanted to make sure it never happened again'.[27] McCarthy recalled: 'I was the captain of course. I went up to the president's room — that year it was Charlie Hanrahan. I said 'We've got a problem here. The southern contingent say [*sic.*] they won't go on the field for *God Save the Queen*'.[28]

The southern players, at the request of Jeffares, disembarked the bus and convened in Room 100 of the hotel for an impromptu meeting with Hanrahan, and two former IRFU presidents and long-time committeemen, Cahir Davitt and Sarsfield Hogan. These were men of considerable influence and repute. Davitt, son of the Land League figurehead Michael Davitt, was President of the High Court and a well-known public figure. Hogan, also a barrister by training, was a senior civil servant, serving as assistant secretary of the Department of Finance.[29] Both men were key figures within the Republic of Ireland's governmental establishment and no doubt possessed sensitive political antennae, an asset that informed their swift reaction to events in Belfast. Moreover, as veteran IRFU officials, they were accustomed to working with Protestant unionists (both of the Ulster and southern origins) and valued the politics of compromise that had facilitated the maintenance, post-partition, of a solitary national governing body and international rugby team for the entire island of Ireland. The officials in Room 100, then, implored the southern contingent to go out for the British national anthem. Mortell remembered the political gravitas of Davitt's appeal:

> He said that he understood and had sympathy for our point of view but he wondered if we had taken into consideration the consequences that would follow on from our actions. He asked if we were aware that one of the only organisations – sporting or otherwise – which had survived intact the partition of our country was the Irish Rugby Football Union, that great sacrifices had been made over the years to ensure that this remained so but if we persisted with our actions it would be the end of rugby union as it presently existed. He pointed out that staunch Ulster Unionists travelled down to Dublin each year and stood to attention for our national anthem but he said that he was in no doubt that these same men would walk away from the IRFU if we persisted with our action. He said that he enjoyed a personal friendship with Mr. de Valera and that our Prime Minister was aware that the Irish Rugby Football Union provided a conduit through which various

actions and suggestions political and otherwise could be tested between the two parts of Ireland. If it were possible for him to contact Mr. de Valera he was quite confident that he would ask us not to proceed with our proposed action. Cahir Davitt wound up his appeal by telling us that if we withdrew our planned action he would give us his word that no other Irish team would ever be faced with a similar dilemma.[30]

The players quickly agreed with Davitt's proposal and boarded the bus to Ravenhill. McCarthy, another speaker in Room 100, recollected:

> The big thing was that it was the last time this situation was ever going to happen because it was the last game in Belfast and everyone knew that. I gave a speech and said that in fifty years' time, when your grandchildren ask you about it, do you want to be remembered as being the team that made this objection when there was every chance that there would be a rift that would split the Ireland team. And I asked whether I was supposed to run out for the anthem with a team of five men.[31]

As will be seen later in this essay, McCarthy's assertion that everyone knew that this was to be the last game at Ravenhill does not chime with other recollections.

Hanrahan, Hogan and Davitt had good reason to fear the implications of any protest by southern players in Belfast. Fuzzy Anderson, a northerner, said that he believed at least two of the Ulster players would have refused to play if the anthem had not been respected. Having recalled being somewhat bemused at the fact that the southern players were holding a meeting, Anderson continued:

> It had been suggested that they could not stand at attention for the national anthem in this foreign land and they wanted to keep

running about playing with the ball. After hearing about this Noel [Henderson] said he would not have played if it [not respecting the British national anthem] had happened and he would have walked off the field and knowing Noel I believe he would. I think Robin [Thompson] would have too.[32]

Henderson's and Thompson's convictions were never tested, however, as the successful (albeit fretful) intervention of the IRFU officials saw the southern players obediently observe the pre-match formalities.[33] Most of the drama that day, it would appear, occurred before the game as Ireland won what was described by the press as 'about the worst international home fans have had to endure for many years' by six points to nil.[34]

A strict and evidently successful cover-up ensued. When full back Robin Gregg, a northerner, was questioned in May 2004 about the incident he insisted: 'This is the first I have ever heard of it'. His apparent ignorance is reinforced by an amusing tale about what those Northern players, waiting for so long on the coach, thought was happening. The tale bears a great similarity to an incident mentioned by Diffley. McCarthy recalled: 'A funny thing is that in the showers afterwards, one of the Northern players, Joey Gaston, came alongside me and said if he'd known we were praying for the Pope he'd have joined in. At that time Pope Pius XII was dying and the Northern players thought we had got off the coach and gone back to the hotel to pray for the Pope'.[35] There was indeed great concern at the time about the Pope's wellbeing and the state of his health was receiving great publicity, though he lived until October 1958. This recollection of McCarthy's bears a great resemblance to Diffley's account: 'The tight-lipped discussions with the recalcitrant players in Belfast that Saturday morning were, according to the story, a source of much puzzlement to the Northern players. It is said that as the team eventually travelled by coach out to the ground one of the Northern players said to his Southern friend: 'You know, if I had known you were holding a prayer meeting I would have been pleased to have joined you, I would have had no religious objections!'.[36]

Jack Kyle, another northerner, was unaware until the 1970s that anything had happened. Admittedly, he was not playing in the Ravenhill game but he was still very much part of the Irish squad and returned to the side for the next season and played on until 1958. Looking back in 2004, he said: 'None of the Northern players knew anything about the incident and it was at least 20 years later before we heard anything about it'. Robin Thompson's brother, Harry, a contemporary player, though not an international, was also unaware of the affair. He, too, looking back fifty years later said: 'I cannot believe it. Certainly Robin never mentioned it to me'.[37] The southerners, for their part, faithfully followed the IRFU's instructions on secrecy. Roe recalled the instructions from the IRFU officials after the incident. He said: 'People began to smell a rat and so the lid had to be put on it. We were told to keep our mouths shut. We were told not to discuss it, not to talk to the Press about it, not to talk to anyone about it – and quite right'.[38] McCarthy's recollection was identical. He remembered: 'We were sworn to secrecy but we never really spoke to the press in those days. It was a closely guarded secret and it never got out'.[39] Irrespective of its direct readership, the fact that the *Irish Press* published details of the controversy in 1963 meant that it was public knowledge just nine years after the event. It seems quite extraordinary, therefore, that the Northern players could claim ignorance of the events and that the southerners could credibly believe that it remained a secret for any considerable length of time.

The IRFU, it seems, pulled something of a stroke when offering the promise that this would be the final occasion in which the southerners would play international football in Belfast. As it happened, no real concession to the southern players was being offered. The financial exigencies of the game dictated that this decision had already been made. Lansdowne Road was much larger and more conveniently situated than Ravenhill and its revenue-generating capacity, therefore, was greater than the Belfast venue. Moreover, with Lansdowne Road's west stand being developed and related costs to be covered, the scheduling of internationals exclusively in Dublin made financial sense. This rationale was summarised shortly after the Ravenhill match in the *Irish Press*:

> A crowd estimated at less than 30,000 watched the game at Ravenhill on Saturday. If that match had been played at Lansdowne Road it would have attracted 8,000 to 10,000 more and over 4,000 more stand tickets at 15 shillings each would have been sold. That means that the Irish Rugby Football Union, which is so heavily in debt, sacrificed an additional £4,000 or more, which it might have had if the match had been played at headquarters. Fortunately both home internationals next year will be played at Lansdowne Road.[40]

Many of the Scotland players that day agreed that Ravenhill was not the ideal venue. Scotland's Grant Weatherstone, Mortell's rival winger, said: 'The whole ground and facilities did not have much to commend it in those days. All in all ... Ravenhill compared unfavourably with Lansdowne Road.'[41] Scotland hooker Robert MacEwen recalled: 'Ravenhill was a rather antiquated ground with limited crowd capacity. The pitch and the turf were poor. There was a deadish, uninspiring atmosphere. It did not compare [with Lansdowne Road or Murrayfield] and presumably this is why it stopped being an international venue. It was rundown ... had quite inadequate team changing facilities and barely adequate toilets or catering for such a relatively large crowd gathering.'[42]

Conclusion

It is difficult to discern the intensity or, indeed, the precise content of the nationalist feelings that influenced the players who pressed most fervently for the demonstration in Belfast that Saturday. While dissatisfaction at a constitutional position that saw partition copper-fastened by the southern state declaring itself a Republic in 1949 followed by the passing of the Ireland Act at Westminster may have been influential, it is likely that the immediate context was more relevant. The shenanigans involving Joe Hughes in 1950 had brought the contested nature of symbolism in Irish rugby to a head and the subsequent media commentary had made it a topic of public debate. The Irish rugby team had to accommodate men from different states, with conflicting national affiliations who owed loyalty to different flags and national anthems. As Roger MacGinty has pointed out: 'Symbols and symbolism can act as a vehicle for the development of an identity bond between individual and the group and for group solidarity'.[43] This can be said of visual symbols such as flags and emblems, and symbolic rituals such as the performance of national anthems at public events. Although there were initial moves among the Southern contingent not to acknowledge British symbols in Belfast that day, these players eventually accepted that such a protest would risk a North-South split. This break would have divided old friends and prevented future rugby generations from enjoying an all-Ireland partnership not achieved in other sporting and cultural spheres. There is an extent, also, to which rugby's middle-class etiquette ensured that the matter was not discussed between players from opposite sides of the border. To this day the IRFU has kept the matter secret.

This essay, ultimately, sheds light on the complex relationship between sport and politics. Outside agencies not only feel the need to politicise people in sport but can also feel the need to de-politicise them. This duality was apparent at Ravenhill where the Southern players were regarded as a politically uniting force while they were on the pitch as part of an all-Ireland team. On the other hand, they were regarded as politically divisive when they considered disrespecting British symbols. In the end a solution was found and rugby again avoided a politically sensitive situation.

8 LOCATING THE CENTRE: IRISH TRADITIONAL MUSIC AND RE-TRADITIONALISATION AT THE WILLIE CLANCY SUMMER SCHOOL

VERENA COMMINS

The Willie Clancy Summer School is the foremost school for Irish traditional music transmission and practice in the annual Irish traditional music calendar. The particular success of the Willie Clancy Week (as it is more commonly referred to) is the result of a synergy of factors, the reverberations of which resonate in a dialectical exchange with the wider community of Irish traditional music practice. In this essay, two inter-related factors which contribute significantly to the production of cultural authority at the school are considered: Firstly, transmission, and the re-traditionalisation of the processes of transmission at the school and secondly, peripherality and how the location of the school, in the west of Ireland, is a constitutive element in legitimating this re-traditionalising process.

Willie Clancy Week

The Willie Clancy Week offers a ten-day long experience and engagement with Irish traditional music. It takes place annually in Miltown Malbay (henceforth Miltown), a small coastal village on the west coast of County Clare, which itself is sited on the south-west coast of Ireland.[1] Workshop-style classes in the core instruments of Irish traditional music, song and dance are given by 'masters of the tradition' to the 1,000 or so participants in the formal and structured part of the school.[2] In facilitating this number of students, the school utilises a variety of locations in Miltown including schools, public halls and houses. The classes take place in intense four-hour periods every morning from Monday to Saturday during the course of the week and recitals, lectures, concerts and céilís are scheduled for the afternoons and evenings. Students who attend the workshops include children and adult learners from all over Ireland and indeed from international locations near and far. Students engage in an apprenticeship, emerging at the end of the week with an enhanced knowledge of the tradition. The school also, however, attracts a much larger cohort of participants who may not be directly involved in the formal elements of the school's schedule. These attend to partake in, or soak up, the atmosphere created by the numerous music sessions that take place throughout the many pubs of Miltown and its environs on what would appear at times to be a twenty-four hour basis. Many of these sessions include the workshop teachers — the 'masters of tradition' amongst their ranks.

For this community of practice, Willie Clancy, the school's namesake, is an uilleann piping hero, whose techniques resonate through the generations of pipers that follow. Central to Willie Clancy's self-narrative is his recourse to the past, driven as he was to recover the music of Garrett Barry, a nineteenth-century west Clare piper, whose music, while unrecorded was mediated to Willie Clancy via his own father, Gilbert Clancy. Willie Clancy's musical consciousness and reflexive self-identification as tradition-bearer, was in no small part due to his aspiration to repair a perceived broken line of west Clare piping, situated within a much wider discourse of desire for cultural purity.[3] During his lifetime, Willie Clancy carefully collected, nurtured and conveyed Garrett Barry's music into the twentieth century and 'was by general acclamation given Barry's hieratic cloak'.[4] He was driven to make a connection to the grand past of west Clare music, even though 'that connection wasn't there to be maintained' as Garrett Barry died in 1899, nineteen years before Willie Clancy was born.[5]

Willie Clancy's legacy, however, extends far beyond this musical recovery. He nurtured the next generation of musicians and anecdotes of his life are peopled with stories of his good-natured generosity and humour. Thus, his enduring fame emanates from his personality as well as his musical productivity. Designating the school in his honour demonstrates Willie Clancy's affective power and the names 'Willie Clancy' and the 'Willie Clancy Summer School' modulate meanings within an Irish traditional music spectrum that range from uilleann piper to icon. His current status is that of musical icon and star, and while these attributes were embedded in his earthly disposition, they have accrued additional meaning over time since his death, heightened by the additional symbolism of the school's name. The title of the school, rather than fixing one cultural meaning to his name, produces instead a cultural text, whose meaning is created and recreated continuously, in dialogue between the school, its attendees, the community of practising musicians (and in particular pipers), and the media. The commemoration of Willie Clancy's legacy as an uilleann piper then, is central to the organisation of the school. Indeed, the musical and social practices of Willie Clancy during his lifetime are vital to the vision the school both creates and celebrates. Additionally during the week, the national organisation for uilleann piping, Na Píobairí Uilleann, organises what is effectively 'a school within a school', providing not just piping tuition, but also workshops in uilleann-pipe making, maintenance and reed-making.[6] While all core instruments of the tradition are taught, the uilleann pipes are thus privileged in multiple ways.

Cultural authority

The Willie Clancy Week can be conceptualised as a continuation of the revivalist impulses fundamental to the origins of both the Gaelic League (in 1893) and more recently Comhaltas Ceoltóirí Éireann. Comhaltas, founded in 1951 and still the main organising body for Irish traditional music, continued the Gaelic League model of using competition as a pivotal revivalist technique. This manifested itself in a series of county and provincial fleadhanna (music festivals based on competition) culminating each summer with Fleadh Cheoil na hÉireann, a major annual event which currently draws over 250,000 people, and has attracted a significant attendance from its inception.[7] In the early 1970s, the founders of the Willie Clancy Week, like many members of Comhaltas, were concerned with the challenges created by competition and the commercialisation and festivalisation of the Fleadh competition festival itself. Like other revivalist projects, both nationally and internationally, Comhaltas suffered criticism for negative outcomes created by competition. Fears were expressed about the narrowing of styles within Irish music as 'winning' styles were imitated and peripheral styles were neglected or lost.[8] An outcome of the competitive process was that cultural authority in many cases was removed from competing practitioners, and transferred to, or co-opted by, a discrete number of revivalists, adjudicators and winners. The contentiousness of cultural authority was not confined to the realm of competition. Commenting on festivalisation and ancillary attendance at the fleadh during the 1960s, Séamus Mac Mathúna deplored the 'guitar-bangers who have 'move[d] in and take[n] over the show' and stated that 'unless drastic changes can be brought about in the next year or so, the fleadh, as we know it, should be scrapped to allow An Comhaltas to get down to more fruitful work for the music'.[9] Eamon Ó Muirí, ex-chairperson of Comhaltas reiterated this fear, stating that the 'organisation will lose its identity in forests of Beatle hair-dos and fleeces of face-fungus'.[10]

These feelings, which represented a widespread anxiety within Comhaltas, engendered by the growing popularity of the Fleadh, were just one of many factors that influenced the establishment of the Willie Clancy Week. Muiris Ó Rócháin, a founding member of the Willie Clancy Week, spoke of the reduction in spaces for music-making at the Fleadh, resulting in the side-lining of musicians and older practitioners in particular. He witnessed first-hand the marginalisation of older musicians during the 1960s and envisaged creating a space for those discomfited by its festivalisation.[11] He saw in the Willie Clancy Week the opportunity to actively facilitate older musicians, and to respect and nurture their preserve of cultural authority. In keeping with this vision, older musicians are actively valued at Miltown each year. One-hundred-year-old west Clare musician Marty O'Keefe, resident of New York since 1943, attended his first Willie Clancy week in 1992 and has barely missed a year since. In the summer of 2012, Marty performed at the graveside tribute to Willie Clancy as well as demonstrating his multi-instrumental prowess at both the fiddle and concertina recitals. Representing both a west Clare and Irish-American heritage, Marty and his music were honoured and embraced by those who heard him, and his performances exemplified a core foundational impulse of the school.[12] While Comhaltas was involved with the organisation of the first Willie Clancy Week, the summer school developed independent status after its first year.[13] Comhaltas perceived itself, as the 'authority, for enlightenment in Irish music', the main organiser of Irish traditional music practice and therefore a key author in constructing the narrative of Irish traditional music.[14] The authorial intent of the Willie Clancy Week, however, was to privilege local 'masters of tradition', valorising Willie Clancy as above all, a west Clare piper and tradition-bearer. Accordingly, there was unwillingness on the part of its organising committee to allow the perceived 'nationalising' organisation, Comhaltas to take control.[15]

Wider cultural flows also impact the school and create implicit corollaries for the maintenance of cultural authority. Barbara O'Connor and others have argued that 'global capitalism controls cultural production', and Ireland's entry into the EC in 1973 (coinciding with the first Willie Clancy week), clearly signals an engagement with the global market place.[16] If the revival of Irish music, under the aegis of the Gaelic League and later Comhaltas, is perceived as the invention of a national tradition against the denationalising influence of neighbouring Britain, the Willie Clancy Week, as a response, situates itself locally within a global cultural society.

Re-traditionalisation

Diarmuid Ó Giolláin uses the term re-traditionalisation to describe 'the re-orientation of traditional cultural production to modern contexts'.[17] Increased global cultural flows inform the re-traditionalisation of cultural practices in their places of origin, reinstating axiological modes of continuity as local masters re-traditionalise performance and transmission, utilising locally embedded resources, skills and knowledge. Though Comhaltas performed a vital role in creating new contexts for the performance practice of Irish traditional music during its first twenty years, its involvement with organised music transmission was minimal during the same period. Consequently, there was a pedagogical gap in the *modus operandi* of Comhaltas. The lynchpin of the Willie Clancy Week is the master-apprentice dyad, in which the school re-traditionalises the process of transmission by privileging the cultural authority of its masters. During the morning workshops, over one hundred individual tutors share their music in classroom settings, opening a point of access to their cultural capital for learners and creating a context that is both traditional and modern.[18] Its traditionality lies in the manner of its explication of Irish traditional music, in which the aural and visual imitation of the master are the primary methods of transmission. However, this traditional explication is swathed in the trimmings of modernity. For example, the concentrated burst of learning is timetabled to fit with the leisure-time schedules of both its participants and tutors, taking place in the first week of the Irish school holidays every July. Digital recording technology supersedes complete reliance on memory in order to remember tunes and while the orality of the learning experience is central, mediation of this experience through a variety of modes is both commonplace and encouraged: tunes committed to memory during the week, will also be saved as texts, through the use of written notation, and now recording technology. This enables students to revert to the master's detail in the afternoon hours during the week of tuition and more importantly, in the months long after the week has passed.

The early years of the school drew extensively on a group of highly regarded, senior, west Clare tradition-bearers. Bobby Casey, Junior Crehan, John Kelly Senior and Joe Ryan were fiddle players from different parts of west Clare all of whom were involved in a teaching capacity early on.[19] With the exception of Junior Crehan, they were no longer resident in County Clare but made the annual pilgrimage to the school, legitimating the school's and their own west Clare legacy in doing so. The classes of those first years did not offer the clear pedagogical role that teachers at the school today assume, yet the basis of learning by imitation was inherent from the start. This involved the masters 'playing away', an organic process of oral transmission but gradually, teaching has developed over the course of the school, to become much more self-reflexive.[20] Denis Liddy, a current teacher at the school, described his youthful experience of these pioneering fiddle classes facilitated by John Kelly Senior and Bobby Casey. In particular, he was struck by the importance attached by the masters, not so much to what they were playing, but to what they were conveying. 'The abiding memory of it was of John Kelly coming in with various versions of the one tune; say, the 'Tempest', "this is Michael Coleman's version, this is my father's version", and then Bobby would have Scully Casey's version'.[21] The aesthetic references in this system of conveyance, demonstrates the inherent dynamic of the taking up and the handing down of culture. The status afforded to these 'masters of tradition' is not self-ascribed, but predicated instead on recognition of the past. Externally however, the constitutive power of the masters, lay and indeed still lies with 'the group which authorises it and invests it with authority', that is, the organisers of the school and the discourse that the school generates.[22] Interestingly, while each of these 'masters' demonstrated their own clearly developed personal style, by virtue of their place of birth and therefore one hundred per cent traceability, their combined idiolects contributed to the performance rubric 'west Clare style'. The ascription of 'west Clare style' brings with it a responsibility for the music-making of future generations which necessitates equal regard for learning appropriately from past generations. Implicit in the musical authenticity stakes of west Clare (or indeed any musical style) is a tension that exists between the sonicity of the past and the acoustics of the future. Within this tension is the perception of west Clare style as geographically rooted in an untainted past and the positioning of these masters as inheritors of that past. As these masters engage in the process of re-traditionalisation, they simultaneously become gate-keepers to the sound of the future.

The imparting of practical knowledge is essential to the teaching process as well as informing a broader system of cultural capital transmission. Field work for this research included attending fiddle classes with James Kelly, son of John Kelly senior, one of the original west Clare masters of tradition.[23] In performative contexts, a fundamental method by which the cultural capital and authority of a master is disseminated resides in their introductions and story-telling narratives, particularly as these relate to tune acquisition and the regime of naming and remembering (and indeed forgetting) tunes. The ultimate story resides in the provenance of any given tune and the master's own placement in that tune's lineage. James Kelly's class narrative strongly acknowledged the presence of his father and other key tradition-bearers. Before teaching the reel 'Last Night's Fun', he recalled how it was popularly played by his father and others along with another tune which he played, but could not recall the name of. James told us that when he was a young boy of ten or eleven years old, 'it got a great going over . . . I remember being in the room listening to that and I thought I was in heaven'.[24] This youthful immersion and unbridled access amplifies the authority that he both bears and represents. Visits to James Kelly's classroom from other masters such as Vincent Griffin and Sean Keane, revealed, in the resulting discourse, that both of these players had taught James at various times, further substantiating his lineage.[25]

Another visiting tutor to the class was a young, American-born fiddle player. In conversation with James, he placed himself into a musical lineage by referencing their shared connection to renowned fiddle player and teacher, Brendan Mulvihill.[26] He prefaced one tune 'Give us another' composed by John McFadden, by associating the musical provenance of John McFadden to the Francis O'Neill cylinders.[27] These cylinders contain some of the earliest recordings of Irish traditional music, and their referencing validates an authoritative yet seemingly effortless engagement with the tradition. This recourse to past masters is recognition of the authority of tradition and an acknowledgement of both belonging to it and representing it. Throughout the one hundred plus workshops taking place at the school, the embodied memories of its teaching masters are transformed, by story and anecdote, from the personal to the public domain. In providing this opportunity for the telling and retelling of stories, the school facilitates the transmission of living memory into cultural memory. In the brief instance outlined here, a casual preamble to performance, reveals a deep signification, thick with cultural content, meaning and explication.

Peripherality

Joe Cleary notes that according to the 1966 census, the urban population of the Republic of Ireland exceeded the rural population for the first time.[28] The urban traditionalising narratives of Comhaltas, and indeed, the recording industry, depicted depopulating rural areas as at the margins, socially, culturally and musically. According to Cleary, 'the marginal culture's destiny is to emulate, it does not inaugurate, initiate or invent'.[29] However, Philip Bohlman evinces the accrual of power that occurs at the periphery or edge.[30] At the time of the Willie Clancy Week's inception in 1973, both Miltown and Irish traditional music shared a common quality, that of peripherality. The site of the school, in County Clare, embodies both the symbolic location of 'the west' and the concept of anchoring a national tradition back in 'the local'. The gathering of Clare masters of traditional music in Miltown, explicitly enunciated 'the local' through style and physical location with a clear remit that through teaching they would share the cultural capital they embodied. Drawing on the success of the national revival of Irish traditional music, spearheaded by the Gaelic League, piping clubs and Comhaltas, the Willie Clancy Week re-traditionalised the local, by moving cultural production, once perceived to be peripheral, back to the centre. Accordingly, the periphery – centre boundary of Irish traditional music converges in Miltown as attention shifts to the constitutive structures and relations of a small town in the animation of Irish traditional music transmission. 'The west' is re-constituted as central, with Miltown at the epicentre of that. Miltown's identity is transformed into a location that continuously re-inscribes Irish music-making practices into its history as invocations of music-making extend far beyond its annual one-week duration.

If an alternative picture could be drawn, one might consider the equally erudite and iconic Dublin piper, Leo Rowsome, who died just a few years before Willie Clancy in 1970. One of the most important outcomes of the foundation of the Dublin Pipers' Club in 1900 is the proliferation and tradition of piping in Dublin that was, and still is, much stronger than that of west Clare. On that basis, one might assume that this makes a strong case for initiating a 'Leo Rowsome Summer School' in Dublin. But the capital city, with its urban backdrop of commerce and materialism, represents the face of a nationalised tradition in contrast to the strongly imagined roots of this music practice in the rural and, more particularly, in the west of Ireland. Situating a comparable school in Dublin has the potential to advance the process of de-traditionalisation.[31]

The idealisation of the west as a cultural heartland is a legacy reiterated by the Gaelic Revivalists who imagined the pure, native landscape of the west of Ireland as representing the Irish nation prior to its Anglicisation. This equation of rurality with true Irishness re-imagines a village like Miltown as a place apart, a haven from modern industrialised society. In reality, factors such as Miltown's inadequate transport connections and infrastructural deficits should mitigate against the success of locating the school there. However, these factors add to a romantic construction of the area in which a traditional Irish culture and way of life survives that contrasts sharply with urban life. The village-level size of Miltown represents a refuge from the hectic pace of everyday life, from which it is imagined to be distanced both spatially and temporally. The traditionalising musical narrative of County Clare has developed within this myth of the west. It is a narrative that advanced in particular from the 1940s onwards with the increasing attention of collectors such as Séamus Ennis, Ciarán Mac Mathúna and later, Tom Munnelly.[32] The county of Clare itself creates a symbolic boundary easily defined geographically and within which the functional status of Irish traditional music is elevated further. The musicianship and personal life story of Willie Clancy solidifies this narrative, which then supports and resounds within the teaching framework of the school and confers cultural authority onto all aspects of the Willie Clancy Week.

Willie Clancy's efforts to concretise the musical legacy of this west Clare community through recovering aesthetic references to Garrett Barry, established a pedigree that was re-sounded by the senior west

Clare fiddle players in the opening years of the school. Drawing on McCann, Bohlman makes the point that 'the centre is not a permanent, unchanging place, rather one that dynamically takes shape and undergoes constant change'.[33] So when this particular cohort of elderly gate-keepers passed away, the school continued to grow and expand, and new gate-keepers emerged. With its own west Clare pedigree firmly and centrally established, the school is in a position to negotiate a space in which other peripheral and local styles can be celebrated. Notably in 1995 an east Clare fiddle workshop was introduced, but more generally, this is now demonstrated by the countrywide and indeed diasporic provenance of the school's tutors. These new inheritors of the 'masters of tradition' status continue to tap into the authority of tradition, and thus appropriate it in order to legitimate their own cultural authority. Throughout each decade of the school, particular attention is paid to the current elder-statesmen of tradition, regardless of their provenance, and their role as important storehouses of indigenous knowledge is privileged. This particular concept is enshrined at the fiddle section of the school in the Archive Room. Situated within the fiddle school, the Archive Room provides a space in which more senior musicians, who no longer teach for the entire week, perform for groups of classes who are invited in during the morning. The activities of the room were initially recorded by the Irish Traditional Music Archive (hence its name). In the last few years, John Joe Tuttle, a west Clare fiddle player and therefore a true local is a mainstay of this room, as is Leitrim musician and elder statesman of Irish music, Ben Lennon, who previously taught for many years at the school.

Other week-long summer schools of Irish music, inspired by the Willie Clancy model, are now claiming, reclaiming and re-traditionalising music-makers and music-practices of their own areas. Continuing throughout the summer, some provide a quieter haven from the intensity of the Willie Clancy Week, but notably nearly all of them are also located along the western seaboard.[34] The school which bears the most resemblance to the Willie Clancy Week, at least in terms of structure and number of students attending workshops, is the annual Scoil Éigse, a week-long Comhaltas sponsored school directly preceding Fleadh Cheoil na hÉireann. Scoil Éigse like the Fleadh itself is a moveable feast and is located in whichever town the Fleadh is taking place in any given year. Whilst both schools attract some overlapping constituencies, Scoil Éigse does not attract the same coterie of annual pilgrims who faithfully attend the Willie Clancy Week. Due to the temporality of Scoil Éigse's location, which shifts every two to three years, in accordance with the Fleadh's mobility, geographically its roots remain shallow. The anonymity of Scoil Éigse fails to enunciate the specific response to individual and collective desire engendered by the man himself, Willie Clancy, and it lacks the focus conveyed by his name. The Willie Clancy Week, which has just celebrated its fortieth year, has garnered an enduring reputation and an unprecedented allegiance amongst the community of practice of Irish traditional music. Due to its location in a town or city large enough to accommodate the Fleadh, its masters and apprentices are unable to colonise spaces in the manner in which Miltown is entirely colonised by the sounds and sights of Irish traditional musicians during the Willie Clancy Week.

Conclusion

Privileging 'the local' is a constitutive feature of the Willie Clancy Week and an alternative to the nationalising narratives attributed to Comhaltas. The school offers a continuum of creative renewal and a dynamic tradition of both taking up and handing down of culture. The process of re-traditionalisation at the Willie Clancy Summer School, draws on stocks of cultural, social and symbolic capital which are held and reinvested in Miltown every year. These stocks are built on a cultural authority, which in turn is predicated on the symbolic significance of the authority of tradition residing in the peripheral location of Miltown

Malbay on the west coast of County Clare. John O'Flynn reiterates Adorno's assertion that 'all aspects of music production and consumption are socially mediated' and draws renewed attention to the concept of nostalgia for the west and the importance of place in constructions of musical authenticity.[35] As the Willie Clancy Week inverts and subverts the periphery-centre dialectic, the school continues to both lead and reflect musical dynamics as it weaves its way through the fabric of Irish music communities and relationships worldwide.

9 LIFE ON-AIR: TALK RADIO AND POPULAR CULTURE IN IRELAND

FINOLA DOYLE O'NEILL

'It used to be the parish pump, but in the Ireland of the 1990s, national radio seems to have taken over as the place where the nation meets'.[1]

This essay will explore the development of talk radio in Ireland, its various inflections and the role of gender in that radio genre. In spite of its popularity in Ireland, radio has in general been under-represented as a field of study. Much research to date has been dominated by analyses of visual media such as film and television and to a lesser extent by a focus on newspapers and magazines. Yet, the development of talk radio as a significant purveyor of popular culture is particularly relevant to an understanding of contemporary Ireland.

Talk radio has introduced new narratives and voices to the Irish public. This genre of radio, which accesses all areas of public discourse, affords Irish audiences, male and female, the opportunity to participate in mass mediated debate and discussion. This was not always the case.

The nineteenth century saw a distinct ideological demarcation between public and private spheres. As men moved out of the home to work and acquired increasing power, the public world they inhabited became identified with influence and control, the private with moral value and support. In bourgeois discourse, this split developed gendered attributes, with men thought 'naturally' to occupy the public arena, while women remained within the domestic and the private, thus excluding them from many areas of public discourse. The nineteenth century also gave rise to a partisan communication model. Newspapers were owned by political parties and candidates and the stream of communication often came from a clearly identifiable source. The late twentieth century, according to Kathleen Hall Jamieson, saw 'a revival of that in the form of talk radio. Political talk radio may be doing the equivalent for political parties that the papers did in the nineteenth century, the partisan newspapers'.[2]

In Ireland, the notion of talk radio as a facilitator of Irish culture began in the form of a public confessional which can be traced back to 1963, with *Dear Frankie*. Frankie Byrne was Ireland's first radio 'agony aunt' and this simple action of unburdening oneself to a relative stranger, albeit through letters and not phone-calls, was to provide the template for not only the *Gay Byrne Show* but also for programmes such as the *Gerry Ryan Show* and RTÉ Radio 1's *Liveline* programme with Joe Duffy. While it is male broadcasters, their listeners are largely female. Women were very much in the home when 'uncle Gaybo' became for many a link to the outside world. In many ways, this was the beginning of the radio-phone-in talk show in Ireland. According to Crisell, the radio phone-in was regarded as a major development in broadcasting. For the first time the listener became an audible presence on the medium, not as a result of her having a letter read out on air or going into studio but 'spontaneously and away from broadcasting equipment, in her own home or local telephone box or at her place of work'.[3] The radio phone-in is a synthesis of private and public media, making it at once 'a private channel of expression and a public forum'[4] and is an inversion of the concept of radio, in that the programme is *about* its audience. This demonstrates that the radio audience can use the medium in many different ways, some talk and some listen, making the relationship between callers and listeners a varied and complex one.

Dear Frankie, broadcast from 1963 to 1985, started out as a domestic science question and answer format on RTÉ radio. Soon it turned into a fifteen-minute programme on relationships that was to run for over twenty years. In many interviews Frankie claimed she knew nothing about domestic science but that she did know about love and so for twenty years Frankie solved the relationship problems of a nation, while hiding the turmoil in her own personal life. Frankie, with her distinctive and husky voice, became a household name in Ireland as the woman who found solutions to problems in a witty yet warm way. The letters received by Frankie, mainly from women, discussed issues such as how to prod a reluctant boyfriend into popping the question and how to get husbands to help out in the home. One such letter, which is certainly reflective of Ireland in a more innocent era, was sent by a woman asking if 'she could get pregnant sitting on her boyfriend's knee?'[5] Frankie Byrne advised her to have a chat with her mother.

Frankie recalled, 'I am interested in people's problems. I am interested in people, you see. I always treat the letters with compassion and understanding'.[6] However, when Frankie gave advice it was according to the RTÉ guidelines of the time. During the 1950s and the 1960s, single mothers, abortion, rape, marital infidelity and condoms were unfit for discussion on air even though they were part of people's lives. Equally unacceptable were queries regarding mental illness, alcoholism, instability or tuberculosis in a family. Those whose questions touched on such matters did not have their problems answered on air. In a rare interview with the *Irish Times* in 1993, Frankie spoke of how heartening it was to see 'the thick fog of hypocrisy lessen'[7] but was sad to note that a lot of the problems remained the same even though they could now be spoken of openly. Frankie was herself a victim of the times and gave a child up for adoption in the 1950s. She spoke of 'the amazingly revealing interviews on the *Gay Byrne Show*', where women would ring in and tell the innermost secrets of their lives. Frankie would listen to these and marvel how things had changed. Many who wrote to Frankie Byrne, wrote to her in despair, printed their letters for fear of recognition and even travelled to different parts of the country to post letters in order to deepen the disguise.

Frankie Byrne died in 1993 at the age of 71. Tributes were led by Gay Byrne who said that for over 'twenty years Frankie Byrne was a national institution who had been loved by everyone'.[8] At its peak the radio show received one hundred letters in a single day from listeners. In more than 1,000 programmes, in which she never missed a week,[9] Frankie, who dealt with almost 5,000 letters, was often quoted as saying that what her listeners wanted was not so much an agony aunt, but a witch doctor with a potion that said 'How to make him love you and stay with you' on the bottle.[10]

By the 1970s in Ireland, alongside the beginnings of *The Gay Byrne Radio Show*, women had made inroads into broadcasting in other areas such as in RTÉ continuity announcement and were highly visible in children's programming. This casting of women's voices as suitable for only particular roles in the public domain is captured in a short rap-style poem 'Men Talk' by the Scottish poet Liz Lochhead.[11] She gives examples of at least fifteen derogatory verbs that relate to female forms of speech. These include 'prattle', 'gossip', 'nag', 'babble' and 'chatter'. Against this list she poses the single linguistic activity of men: 'talk'. According to Myra MacDonald, this differentiation by gender 'filters through into judgements about media genres' and 'attitudes to male and female voice pitch have also been a peculiarly powerful tool where and when men and women might be granted speaking rights within the media'.[12]

The launch of Marian Finucane's *Women Today* programme in 1979 was a landmark broadcasting decision. The programme continued until 1985 on RTÉ Radio 1, after which Finucane took up her afternoon slot as presenter of the new *Liveline* show. Often, it seemed however that Finucane was the solitary female voice. Areas of broadcasting that might have increased the airing of women's voices in a redrafting of private/ public boundaries were (and continue to be in some respects) slow to do so. In Ireland, both the television talk show and the DJ-led programmes on radio, in their straddling of public and private discourse, might have seemed fertile ground for more female presenters. Instead, one glance at the programme schedules for RTÉ Radio 1 for December 2011 would seem to indicate that female presenters are quite scarce in talk show and DJ formats during the weekday schedule. However, each female presenter, though few in number, present the bulk of the news and current affairs output each day. At 7.00am, Rachel English is part of the *Morning Ireland* team, Mary Wilson fronts the evening news magazine programme *Drivetime* and Claire Byrne fronts *The Late Debate* at 10.00pm later that evening.

In 2009, journalist Pól Ó Conghaile posed the question whether women were an endangered species on Ireland's national airwaves?[13] The mainstream overall schedules on national radio may be short on female presenters but conversely, at executive levels, women are well represented in Irish radio and television. In 2009, Ana Leddy was Head of *Radio 1* and Claire Duignan was RTÉ Television's Director of Programmes, while female producers and researchers feature heavily behind the scenes.

In 2008, one of Ireland's top female radio broadcasters, Finucane, was moved to a weekend morning time slot and currently the weekend schedule on RTÉ radio 1 is dominated by two female presenters, Finucane and her colleague, Miriam O'Callaghan. The programmes are a mixture of current affairs, talk show and light entertainment. Finucane's move to the weekend slot may have been a step towards attracting and indeed accommodating a wider cohort of listeners. However, at the music driven RTÉ 2FM, the situation is very different. As a corollary to this, most of the major weekday radio talk shows in Ireland are still hosted by men. *Newstalk 101,* which was the exception, removed two of its top female presenters, Orla Barry and Brenda Power, from its weekday schedules to facilitate the transfer of veteran broadcaster Tom Dunne from *Today FM* to host his own talk show in 2008. It is noteworthy, that women DJs are finally on the increase both at weekends and throughout the weekly schedule on the public broadcasting airwaves, reflecting a consistent pattern throughout all of the twenty-one commercial radio stations in Ireland.

In the United States national public radio presenters have fifty per cent representation by women. In Ireland, the continuing gender imbalance is borne out in a recent survey conducted by the National Women's Council of Ireland (NWCI) into the participation and representation of women's voices in the broadcast media. The survey took current affairs radio programming as its case study. The results of the survey show that on average, less than one-quarter of voices on air are women.[14] The survey, conducted on 1 March 2012, highlights that RTÉ Radio 1's flagship lunchtime radio show, *News at One*, was at the lowest level for women's participation whereby just 12.5% of voices were women. The male presented *Right Hook* on *Newstalk* and the female presented *Marian Finucane Show* (on Sunday) are the best performing shows for women's participation. This research by the NWCI illustrates that women 'continue to be marginalised from current affairs broadcasting, forming just over one-fifth of on air voices in news and current affairs programmes'.[15]

Research by Professor Francis Lee at the Department of Communication at Stanford University has recently written of the significance of the radio phone-in as a forum for public deliberation and as a form of info-tainment that displaces 'serious' political journalism. Taking the highly politicised city of Hong-Kong as his case study, Lee argues that talk shows provide political information to listeners and serve as a forum to criticise the government.[16] On the *Gay Byrne Show*, which aired on RTÉ Radio 1 from 1973 to 1998, Byrne endlessly criticised the government and its running of the country. His constant use of the word 'banjaxed' and 'washed out' were used to refer to the abysmal economic state of Ireland during the 1970s and the 1980s. Byrne's criticism of the work of Irish politicians was challenged in the Dáil by former Cork deputy Bernard Allen who claimed that 'Mr Byrne had grossly insulted members of the house'.[17] Deputy Allen wrote to Mr Jim Culliton, then chairman of the RTÉ Authority, to make a formal complaint. The matter was then referred to the Dáil Committee on Procedure and Privileges. Deputy Allen, who, in a later statement invited Mr Byrne to spend time with him in his Cork north-central constituency, remarked that 'Gay Byrne has undoubtedly opened up for national debate many issues which need to be confronted. Unfortunately, he has also contributed to a growing sense of cynicism, particularly about politicians'.[18]

In the United States, revelations by the host on both political and personal matters have transformed talk radio into a cultural and political phenomenon. Radio hosts such as Rush Limbaugh and G. Gordon Liddy are woven into the very fabric of American popular culture and their shows operate as potent political tools. The acknowledgement of political influence in this kind of programming began more transparently in the USA when the Federal Communications Commission repealed the Radio Fairness Doctrine in 1987. Under the previous doctrine, all political views had to be accorded equal representation on the airwaves. With the doctrine's repeal, talk radio became more opinionated and more unbalanced, leading to controversial talk show hosts such as California's Limbaugh gaining huge listenership figures. The popularity of the talk radio show in America is evidenced by its phenomenal growth from 1990 with 400 shows nationwide to 1400 shows in 2007.[19]

This notion of radio as a confessional was also evident, albeit in a much lighter vein, with the emergence of Terence, the agony uncle, on the *Gerry Ryan Show* on RTÉ 2FM in the 1980s. Described, tongue-in-cheek by an *Irish Times* radio critic as a cross between 'Woody Allen, Liberace, Max Headroom and Frank Spenser of *Some Mothers Do 'Ave 'Em*'[20] this 'flamboyant but tragic Chaplinesque figure on the broadcasting landscape'[21] rose to prominence while still working as a 'hairdresser' in Cork. He would phone in to the *Gerry Ryan Show* and simultaneously regale and entertain listeners with advice and absurd opinions. Terence, alias veteran broadcaster, John Creedon, was the radio doppelganger of the BBC television drag queen, Dame Edna Everage and was endearing with his childlike catchphrase 'We're all God's children'. For radio listeners in Ireland in the late 1980s, Terence was the champion of the underdog as he meted out questionable advice to his chosen target audience, the housewives and the unemployed. He was an entertaining interlude in an Ireland not yet gripped by the sophistication that the Celtic Tiger would herald. When the 1990s did come into view, Terence and his simplistic and childlike philosophy became redundant.

Today, satellite and digital transmission has turned talk radio into a vigorous and political force. Radio phone-in shows on which listeners express their views, have become quick shapers of public opinion and can provoke endless controversy. In America, the political impact of talk radio is particularly apparent. In the 1990s, right-wing Christian groups exploited the power of the radio talk show to generate much of the opposition to President Clinton's plan to lift the ban on the recruitment and retention of homosexuals in the military forces. Studies show that in America, talk shows on black, Hispanic, and Asian radio stations have an especially strong social impact,[22] surmounting language and cultural barriers to deliver important information to their audiences. For example, urban black radio stations conducted AIDS Awareness Days for their listeners when it was revealed, in 1994, that Earvin 'Magic' Johnson, the Los Angeles Laker basketball star, disclosed that he had tested positive for the HIV virus.

The *Gerry Ryan Show* on 2FM, which began in 1988, provides a good example of an enduring radio talk show that was a new departure in the Irish radio landscape. His former RTÉ website stated:

> Gerry likes to talk and so do the Irish ... Gerry looked to his new audience for their thoughts and opinions on everything from unemployment to underpants. Nothing is too sacred. Not anymore. If you need to talk about it, you need to talk to Gerry.[23]

From the very start, Gerry Ryan became master of the intimate conversation and was beginning to worry Gay Byrne who claimed in an *Irish Times* interview in September 1988 that 'we are all dipping into the same bucket and people will react against it'. Byrne seemed rattled by Ryan, the then 32-year-old former rock DJ with the ponytail. Since his three-hour programme began in March 1988 up until his untimely death due to a heart attack in April 2010, Ryan enjoyed a large market share of the audience due to his charismatic presence, offbeat fascinations and sexual innuendos. Ryan, who claimed he liked to think of talk radio as 'eavesdropping on dirty talk'[24] was Gay Byrne for those under thirty-five. In the late 1980s Ryan had seized a market where consumers wanted their talk sexier, brasher and more and more emotionally intense. Based on the US-style of radio known as Zoo Radio, a vibrant, irreverent and unpredictable style of radio presentation,[25] Ryan proved to be more liberal, more urban and more colloquial in style than Byrne and this added to his appeal for younger audiences. Ryan, back in 1988, commented on the unpredictability of radio and the rush to the airwaves by listeners wanting their voices to be heard, an observation which still rings true in the twenty-first century:

> It's that magical mixture of debating sensitive issues like health cuts or adoption one minute then suddenly you find yourself in some mad discussion about battery chickens. And it's also democratic radio from the point of view that people are given a platform to air their views. Irish people don't complain to their TDs or to the relevant service or authority, yet they will come on air because the

radio is there and say: damn it, all I have to do is lift the phone and tell Gerry Ryan about it.[26]

Ryan's candid telephone techniques, in the early years, landed him in hot water. On a programme in October 1989 he phoned the Department of the Environment live on air, seeking advice on how to dispose of his fridge without damaging the ozone layer. The questionable ethics of putting an official live on air without their knowledge or permission, was the stuff of Ryan's tabloid radio style, a style quite contrary to Byrne's avuncular and traditional approach. By 1990, Ryan had defeated Byrne in catching the 16-54-year-old age group in the Dublin area.[27] The show took on the quality of an addictive soap opera, with its regular contributors such as Terence the agony uncle, the three barflies who talked in tangents, and dietician Denise Sweeney who would drop in for daft competitions such as a 'smell the cheese' phone-in. In contrast, Gay Byrne would read out twenty letters per programme from listeners, in a dry, safe way, interspersed with funny voices; Ryan rarely used letters but let the stream of phone calls shape and mould the show, a riskier style of broadcasting that yielded huge dividends.

In the early 1990s local radio began to pose a serious challenge to both the *Gay Byrne Show* and the *Gerry Ryan Show*. Former director of local radio station *LMFM*, Gavin Duffy, recalls how Paul Claffey of Midwest Radio began to make a breakthrough by opening his talk radio show with death notices. Soon all local radio stations began broadcasting death notices from 9.00am to compete with Gerry Ryan and Gay Byrne. Irked by the loss of listeners from the first half of his programme, Ryan decided to devote an entire programme to death notices and death and asked callers to ring in with their dream funeral arrangements. Gavin Duffy recounts the response to this particular programme:

Along with those wishing to have their ashes cast over the Cliffs of Moher, or to be buried under the goalposts at Croke Park, was a gem – a caller infamously declared his dream internment would be to be buried up to his bollocks in Bibi Baskin.[28] Long before Twitter or the net, the entire nation was abuzz that day, everyone asking 'did you hear the guy on the *Gerry Ryan Show*?' King Gerry had wrestled back his crown from the local radio pretenders.[29]

Up until his final show on Thursday 29 April 2010, over thirty years on air, twenty-two of them with his own day-time talk show, Gerry Ryan brought in huge audience figures of often over half a million listeners, in spite of the stiff competition from local radio stations and latterly national commercial stations. Ryan would calculatedly admit or feign ignorance on any subject before becoming an instant expert. He was once described as a 'fast-talking, jumpy, fidget of a man who will reach out and spin the chair next to him while he airs his views on Irish society'.[30] This is the same Ryan who also featured prominently on RTÉ television with programmes such as *The School Around the Corner*, *Operation Transformation* and *Ryan Confidential,* a series of intimate interviews with well-known celebrities. His early death at the age of 53 caused public outpourings of grief and his funeral mass was broadcast live on *RTÉ 2FM*. According to one media commentator, Gerry Ryan's funeral, like his radio persona, broke all the rules:

> There was a small church for a giant personality, reverential tones for the king of irreverence, mild jokes for a raucous sense of humour and minimal embellishment for the most flamboyant of characters.[31]

While the 1990s in particular embraced the raucous exhibitionism of Gerry Ryan, the millennium became the decade of a less flamboyant genre of public confessional in the format of the radio-phone in show *Liveline,* presented by Joe Duffy, a former *Gay Byrne Show* co-host and a protégée of the eponymous man. In 1999, now deceased journalist

Jonathan Philbin Bowman wrote:

> Who is the most powerful man in the country ... Bertie Ahern? Wrong. The new centre of power in our now whingocracy is in RTÉ's Radio building, from where Joe Duffy dispenses justice, favours and distils demands each weekday from 1.45.[32]

Liveline, on RTÉ Radio 1, is now part of Ireland's popular culture and in fact has arguably helped shape the nation's political and cultural landscape. In 2008 Joe Duffy was accused by former Fianna Fail Finance Minister Brian Lenihan, of 'eliciting public opinion' on the financial turmoil that gripped the country at that time. Duffy was attacked by the Minister for 'provoking unprecedented panic'[33] amid general fears that it might lead to a run on the banks. Significant sums were believed to have been removed from the banks subsequent to the *Liveline* programme of 19 September 2008, when an estimated €50 million was lodged to An Post's state-guaranteed savings scheme in just one 24-hour period. A senior figure in Irish banking reported to the *Sunday Independent* that 'the *Liveline* programme on Thursday, 19 September, was absolutely its single most destructive broadcast ever'.[34] On 14 September 2009, Duffy interviewed Irish TV scriptwriter Frank Deasy (who died shortly after the interview was broadcast). He told listeners that his need for an organ donor had become 'very urgent'. Mr Deasy's appeal to carry organ donor cards resulted in more than 5,000 people applying to the Irish Kidney Association to carry these cards.[35]

In contrast to the *Gay Byrne Show*, which of its day was new as a form of public confessional, talk radio shows such as *Liveline* and the *Gerry Ryan Show* saw the advent of the mobile phone precipitate the volume of callers phoning in to talk about intimacies previously discussed in private, or not at all. The national confessional also developed locally with the advent of commercial local radio beginning in 1988. The diversity of culture in Ireland was immediately apparent as listeners tuned into their own local radio stations to discuss problems and issues specific to their locality. Cork's *96FM* and its *Opinion-line* with Neil Prendeville is an example of how radio can reflect diversity. According to the *96FM* website, 'When Cork people talk, they talk to Neil Prendeville … sometimes controversial, sometimes touching, but always crucial listening'.[36] *Radio Kerry*, voted best local/regional radio station of the year in 2007, is another example of the ability of local radio to monitor the heartbeat of a community. *Kerry Today*, presented by Deirdre Walsh, 'is the county's number one radio programme — it is passionate about Kerry and its people — *Kerry Today* is the show to break the news and to deliver the stories that matter to our listeners'.[37] Radio Listenership Figures for June 2010 to June 2011 indicate that talk radio hosts such as Joe Duffy and Marian Finucane both recorded double-digit growth in their audience size for 2011, with Joe Duffy's *Liveline* standing at 400,000.[38] The public's appetite for hearing its own voice on the airwaves evidently remains strong.

Today, talk radio's moment-to-moment unpredictability has been somewhat diminished by the necessity to weed-out libellous, harassing or repeat callers. This is achieved by almost seamless live editing techniques that nonetheless restrain most of radio's rough spontaneity and realism. Many radio hosts now have the benefit of a call-screener or a digital delay system. This prevents the programme from being aired for four to five seconds so that, with the push of a 'dump button' any operator may delete a profanity, personal attack, libel or copyright infringement. In addition, twenty-four hour logged tapes, give the station a record of the programme in the event of legal action or complaints arising. However, it is these very elements of chance, fostered by call-in participation, which has given the format its uniqueness, its element of surprise, its drama, and its unrivalled appeal.

Unpredictability connotes a sense of credibility vital to the effectiveness of the talk radio genre. This was in evidence on the 1 May 2007 edition of *Liveline* where host Joe Duffy received a surprise call from an inmate in one of Ireland's state prisons. The inmate in question was criminal John Daly, now deceased. His easy access to the national airwaves led to a storm of media protest regarding the outlawing of mobile phones in state prisons and the lack of vigilance regarding their use by prisoners within the state system.

Talk radio also makes for a productive instability, a use of chaos, that allows it to stand out against the tight predictable formulas of current affairs and music programmes, in fact the whole formulaic array of popular culture. BBC Radio's 'honorary' Irishman, Terry Wogan is a good example of 'productive instability' at its best in the way that he 'spiced with the best of Irishness the Englishness he fell in love with as a boy listening to the BBC'.[39] In September 2009 'a cloud of melancholy descended on eight million or so listeners to BBC Radio 2's *Wake Up To Wogan*'[40] when the 71-year-old Limerickman and veteran broadcaster announced his retirement from his radio talk show. Wogan, who made an art of the genial insult and who used his listener's comments as a form of programme script, was the recipient of an honorary degree from the University of Leicester for his outstanding charity work and his 'contribution to British culture'.[41] The self-deprecating decency of Wogan's style of talk radio is in sharp contrast to the open-line talk radio shows, which are notorious for generating a high degree of controversial and confrontational talk between their hosts and the callers, who, for the most part, are ordinary citizens.

The Irish radio talk show is far less confrontational than its US counterpart. The popularity of talk radio in the US was evidenced by the release of the 1980s movie, *Talk Radio*. The film centred around the daily life and work of a controversial talk radio host whose character, although fictional, was loosely based on a real-life US radio host, Alan Berg. The controversy generated through his show resulted in him being shot by a vengeful listener. In the 1940s German playwright Bertolt Brecht suggested that 'radio would be the finest possible communication apparatus in public life, a vast network ... That is to say, it would be if it knew how to receive as well as to transmit, how to let the listener speak as well as hear, how to bring him into a relationship instead of isolating him'.[42] These possibilities are now realised in the radio talk show. The democratic possibilities of talk radio are realised in an Irish context when Gay Byrne or Gerry Ryan, facilitated open debate between themselves and members of the public.

In 1995, Gerry Ryan stated that the case of the paedophile priest, Fr Brendan Smyth, had more of a dramatic effect on talk radio than any other single event:

> There has been a complete change in the attitude of middle Ireland to talking about the faults of the Catholic Church. Eight years ago you would not have heard middle-aged women, who were still regular mass-goers, coming on radio to complain about 'that shower' in Maynooth or whatever. But it's happening now.[43]

Luke Gibbons believes the watershed event in the development of talk radio was Gerry Ryan's interview with Lavinia Kerwick, after the man convicted of her rape walked free from the Central Criminal Court in Dublin with a suspended sentence. Gibbons interprets her interview on national radio as a defining event, both for women, and for the medium.[44]

It is worth noting that the *Gay Byrne Show,* unlike much of today's talk radio programmes, was never openly confrontational. RTÉ's *Liveline,* for example, thrives on caller phone-in disagreements and confrontations. The *Gay Byrne Show* was not, in principle, talk radio, but rather a radio programme which facilitated talk. It also reflected contemporary Ireland in its choice of newspaper clippings, letters to the show, as well as the listener phone-ins and their comments. According to former producer John Caden:

> In the period when the *Gay Byrne Show* was clocking up three quarters of a million listeners a day, the issues of the times were the

way people were won over to it, and there's no doubt about that. I'm absolutely convinced that there's an insatiable desire in this country for serious, well-conducted, lively entertaining debate.[45]

Paddy Scannell sees talk radio as a 'form of institutional interaction'.[46] The talk takes place within an organisation, the broadcasting company. At the same time, however, the institutional space in which talk radio interactions take place is somewhat unique. It is a space created at the interface of private and public spheres of modern society. In calls to talk radio shows, for example, *Liveline*, a specialised form of talk about personal opinions of public issues is produced by two individuals respectively occupying what Scannell described as 'completely separate … places from which broadcasting speaks and in which it is heard'.[47] For the most part, in broadcasting, the studio represents the primary location from which broadcast talk emerges: it is 'the institutional discursive space of radio and television'. [48] Listening and viewing, on the other hand, 'take place in the sphere of domesticity, within the spaces of the household and normatively in the small family living room'.[49]

On talk radio, the voices of ordinary people are carried from that domestic sphere into the institutional space of the studio, and then projected back again, via the radio, to the domestic sphere of the audience. It is the uniqueness of this discursive space of talk radio that makes it such an important aspect of popular culture. In September 2011, Joe Duffy's *Liveline* had listenership figures of 423,000, an increase of 45,000 listeners from September of the previous year.[50] The figure reflected the success of this radio phone-in show genre. The success of *Liveline* highlights the fact that talk radio is still a phenomenally popular choice of public discourse in Ireland. In 1973, when the *Gay Byrne Show* first began, no one could have imagined that a one-hour radio programme targeted at women in the home would have metamorphosed into an oftentimes painful and revealing journey through popular Irish culture for over 26 years and would set the template for the talk radio genre. The

Gay Byrne Show aired at a time in Ireland's cultural history when simply airing social and personal relationship problems was in itself a socially revolutionary activity.

Today, with 85 per cent of adults in Ireland tuning into radio on a daily basis,[51] talk radio is an important cultural phenomenon within the Irish media landscape. Radio has a tradition that extends right back to the foundations of the state. During those earlier years of sponsored programming, radio did not reflect popular culture but rather adhered to the Reithian principle of giving the people, not what they wanted, but rather what the state felt they needed. And so there were army bands, traditional musicians, programmes in Irish and how to teach Irish. Back then the schedule was predictable and safe. There was news and current affairs, radio drama and the excellent Thomas Davis lecture series. There was Frankie Byrne, Irish radio's first agony aunt and then in 1973, came, what was essentially a housewives programme – the *Gay Byrne Show.* This became the heartbeat of popular culture in Ireland. More change was to occur when, in 1989, pirate radio was regularised and the first wave of national and local independent radio stations began broadcasting to regional audiences starved of local references and resonances.

The reluctant establishment of the Independent Radio and Television Commission (now the Broadcasting Commission of Ireland, or BCI), by Minister for Communications, Ray Burke, held out the prospect of some twenty or more local FM stations covering every town, city and country, as well national competitors to RTÉ. Today there are over twenty-four local independent stations, one 'pan-regional' station (Beat FM), seventeen special interest or community stations and two national independent operators (Newstalk and Today FM). In 2007, new licences were awarded to youth stations in the south-west, north-west and the north-east/midlands area. This is in addition to RTÉ's four national commercial channels, *Radio 1, 2FM, Radio Na Gaeltachta* and *Lyric FM.*

In spite of the proliferation of local radio stations, *Liveline,* on RTÉ Radio 1 is the most popular talk show nationally on Irish radio.[52] The popularity of this genre of radio is worthy of further study. Its history can be traced back to Gay Byrne and his uniquely Irish adaptation of the talk radio genre in 1973. His uniquely formatted radio programme, the *Gay Byrne Show* acted as both a catalyst for change and as a barometer of Ireland's cultural transformation throughout its years on air. In twenty first century Ireland, talk radio continues to be a quintessential aspect of popular culture. The confession box has for many, lost both its spiritual and intimate appeal. A new congregation is now flourishing – the radio talk show devotee. When in need of guidance or merely wish to gripe — talk to Joe. He and over 400,500 people are listening!

10 NEITHER WHITE NOR FREE: IRISH RAILROAD WORKERS IN THE TROUBLED COLONY OF CUBA, 1835–1837

MARGARET BREHONY

The Spanish colony of Cuba is not a destination usually associated with Irish migration; however, it has had its share of Irish merchants, soldiers, settlers and migrant labourers throughout its colonial history. This essay examines an account, as recorded by the Cuban colonial authorities, of a 'colony' of *irlandeses*, contracted in New York in 1835, to work on the construction of the Cuban railroad, the first in the Spanish empire. Irish workers were introduced into the ranks of an incipient proletariat in an expanding slave system under threat of abolition, becoming part of a multi-ethnic workforce of indentured labourers from the Canary Islands, and enslaved African and Creole labourers. Forced into a brutal work regime akin to slavery, under Spanish military rule, any attempt to escape was treated as desertion, punishable by prison or execution. The archival documents referring to Irish immigrants in Cuba are treated here, not as a 'repository of the facts' but, more as a 'complexly constituted' discourse of slavery and free labour, produced in the formation of colonial processes of class, ethnicity and migration.[1]

Irish contract labourers became part of a modernising project to replace slavery with 'free' labour with the additional aim of 'whitening the population'. An account by David Turnbull, British Consul to Cuba at the time, locates this mobile 'reserve army' of industrial capitalism as follows:

> … to show how much could be done for little money, upwards of a thousand Irishmen, who are to be found in every part of the world prepared with their lusty sinews to cheapen the price of labour, were tempted in an evil hour to go there [Cuba] from the United States, allured by promises on the part of the railroad company, which were never fulfilled.[2]

In 1835, when international pressure to abolish slavery in Cuba was as its height, Irish immigrants were applauded by colonial elites as an ideal substitute for slave labour in the formation of a proletarian underclass. However, protest and rebellion by the railroad workers led to their early repudiation by the authorities disrupting an earlier discourse about Irish Catholics as victims of British colonialism, as likely 'whitening agents' in stemming the 'africanisation' of Cuba. In a new discourse of transition to 'free' labour, recalcitrant railroad workers were viewed as a risk to the economic imperatives of sugar production; described as 'turbulent and feckless' and 'indifferent to the rewards of labour', they became a threat to the social order. This essay argues that the violent relationship which developed between Irish migrant labour and capital on the Cuban railroad eclipsed expectations of religious or race solidarities and gained ascendancy over an imagined Irish potential in the inscription of whiteness. The case of the Irish railroad workers in Cuba is examined here in light of the reformulation of ethnicity in the discursive strategies of the sugar planter elite as it reflects the reformulation of labour relations.

Records of Irish immigrant lives in Cuba appear mainly in the manuscripts of the colonial bureaucracies responsible for the construction of the railroad and in documents of the Council for White Population (*Junta de Población Blanca*) responsible for the promotion of 'white colonisation' strategies. A poor, transient and often illiterate cohort, this group of Irish migrants left no first hand records of their experiences. However, they make their presence felt in the documents of the earliest railroad construction through their resistance to the coercions of a highly racialised system of colonial labour. In the historiography of the railroad, Cuban historians pay tribute to Irish migrants, as some of the first large-scale importation of wage labourers into the Spanish colony, for their contribution to labour history and working-class struggle. In his pioneering study of sugar and slavery, *The Sugarmill,* Moreno-Fraginals described the Irish imports as 'a morally and physically degraded lumpen proletariat' and victims of colonial neglect. In the most extensive historical work on the Cuban railroad, they are described as 'victims of wage-labour', 'hardened drunks and turbulent individuals', this time in the Spanish empire.[3] This first Irish account contextualises their position within the overlapping processes of class, race and labour in Cuba in the 1830s within the colonial discourse of 'free', 'white' and 'waged'. Attempts by colonial elites to engineer the racial demographics of labour, by substituting slave labour with 'free' white labour, were tempered by the reluctance on the part of Cuba's slave-owners to relinquish a sense of ownership of labour. It was also challenged in this instance by a mobile proletariat with a track record of resistance to colonial capitalism originating in the agrarian underground of pre-famine Ireland and honed in the industrial centres of North America.

Sugar, Slavery and 'Whitening' the Cuban Nation

Cuba, by 1835, was still tied to the Spanish empire in a colonial relationship that was maintained in exchange for the protection of a slave system. At a time when most other societies were turning away from slavery and sugar production, Cuba was belatedly emerging as the most advanced large-scale sugar industry the world had ever seen. To increase production the colony's wealthy sugar-producing elite invested in the 'sugar-railroad', linking the rich plantations of the Güines Valley with the port of Havana. The railroad provided a cheaper, faster route to the global market, but also opened the way for profound economic transformation. The resulting industrialisation and increased prosperity copper-fastened Cuba's dependence on sugar and on slavery in one of Spain's last colonial possessions. The implications for Cuban society were equally transformative, particularly in the hardening of caste-like hierarchies of race and labour relations and the 'racially bifurcated principle of governance'.[4] With a population of 700,000 in 1827, of which 41 per cent were enslaved, continued large-scale importation of forced African labour in the early decades of the nineteenth century which, when combined with free blacks, resulted in a majority black population reaching 61 per cent of the total by 1841. Evoking the spectre of a black independent republic in neighbouring Haiti, Alexander Humboldt, in 1826, cautioned against the system of slavery:

> If the laws in the Antilles and the legal status of people of colour do not change for the better soon and if we continue to talk without acting, political supremacy will pass into the hands of those who have the power of labour, the will to emancipate themselves, and the courage to endure long privations.[5]

Such 'dangerous' sentiments were censored by the Cuban authorities and a dynamic clandestine slave trade continued up to the 1860s. Demographics, labour relations and national identity dominated political and economic debates and the discourse of anti-slavery overlapped with anti-colonial sentiment – albeit with racist undertones. Black insurgency in the struggle for independence gave rise to the concept of a 'raceless nationality' – in the words of the most popular leader, Antonio Maceo who in the war against Spain stated a desire for a nation with 'no whites nor blacks, but only Cubans'.[6] As Turnbull observed 'The great object of Creole patriots is to increase the white population, and thus render further importation of Africans unnecessary. Without denying them the credit of Philanthropic motives, it cannot be concealed that the desire for independence may be traced through all their reasoning'.[7]

The Spanish Crown, concerned that the advocates of abolition were also advocates of independence from Spain, continued to turn a blind eye to the illegal slave trade, believing that the fear of another Haiti strengthened the ties of the 'ever-faithful isle' to the metropolis. Abolition did not sit comfortably with slave-holding nationalists, fearing insurgence 'from below' and the threat it posed to their economic life-blood. Concerned to protect their wealth and status within Empire, reform-minded creoles amongst Cuba's modernising elite conceived of a nation racially and culturally in their own likeness populated by Europeans and their descendants. In a society faced with abolition and the prospect of sharing citizenship with people of colour (*gente de color*) the Spanish preoccupation with 'purity of blood' (*limpieza de sangre*) moved to an expression of nationality that 'gradually evolved into an unwritten law of purity of the skin to reinforce white supremacy'.[8] José Antonio Saco, the 'apostle' of Cuban nationalism argued that 'miscegenation was the only viable means' of ensuring that the emerging Cuban nation would become lighter over time.[9] Saco decried slavery, not on any moral grounds, but in unequivocally racist terms he argued that it was an obstacle to 'progress and civilisation'; and in economic terms it was 'a hydra that frightens those capitalists who would come to settle on our soil'.[10] Saco's proto-nationalism, in which he saw slavery as the cornerstone of Spanish colonial domination, expressed an ardent desire to bring about '*la disminución, la extinción si fuera posible, de la raza negra*' (to diminish or if possible extinguish the black race) before it ruined 'our island' economically and culturally.[11] Saco's prescription for white-washing the population, while ensuring the protection of class and white racial purity, would confine such mixing to free black women and poor white immigrants. The 'pure white' woman of the Creole elite, who stood in contrast to the 'almost white' *mulata* (mulatta, a woman of mixed-race), would not be contaminated in the creation of a white under-class. In this case the union of 'not quite white' Irish labourers with Afro-Cubans would not only provide bodies for a substitute labour force, it would bolster the nation's racial project of *blanqueamiento* (whitening) while ensuring a class ceiling, in what Guevara calls the 'ultimate unattainability of whiteness by non-whites'.[12] The colonial category of *mestisaje* (interracial unions), as argued by Stoler, embodies one of the tensions of empire, that of inclusion/exclusion, which in colonial Cuba turned on Creole/Spanish credentials as well as on racial categories. Included as labouring bodies in the project of nationhood, but excluded from 'white prestige', the boundaries and privilege of those who conceived the policy, Cuban (descendants of European) white males, would be assured.[13] The project of *blanqueamiento* or 'whitening' the nation was constructed in social and cultural terms, in opposition to what was termed 'africanisation', and rested on a modernising imperative and rhetoric of economic progress. Contamination of class was protected through surveillance of the 'white woman' of the elite ruling class and contamination of race was protected by policing sexual contact through legislation. Guevara argues that miscegenation 'was sanctioned only when it involved women of colour and white men, thus adhering to a legal system that limited inter-racial marriage to poor white men and women of colour'.[14] This is borne out by the records that show a high number of inter-racial unions between impoverished white immigrant men and free black and mulatto women.[15]

The abolition of slavery in the neighbouring British West Indies in 1833 and the second Anglo-Spanish Treaty, signed in 1835, exerted renewed international pressure on the Spanish Crown to end the trade in slaves. The threat of abolition pushed the search for labour in new directions to recruit cheap immigrant labour and in line with the new dictates of political economy the planters voiced a willingness to introduce 'free' labour in the search for a substitute for slavery. Dovetailing with the labour demands of the railroad, the Royal Development Council (*Junta de Fomento*) was charged with adopting measures to give 'occupation to useful labourers from the Peninsula, its adjacent islands, or from other points in Europe'.[16] The colonial authorities set about incorporating immigrant contract labour from Ireland, the Canary Islands, Galicia and finally China into an entrenched system of slavery that continued until the last decades of the nineteenth century. The resulting labour system introduced new forms of coercive practices and racial hierarchies, which functionally were not much different to slavery, but served nominally at least in tipping the balance in favour of the white population.

The Royal Development Council became like an 'ambidextrous gambler' combining the importation of white wage-labourers with the rental of any available surplus slaves.[17] Towards the end of 1834 the Council secured an initial loan of two million dollars from a London banking firm. The Spanish Consul in New York, Francisco Stoughton, contracted American engineers Alfred Kruger and Benjamin Wright Jr. to direct the construction of the railroad. Excavations to lay the tracks of the first twenty-nine mile stretch of railroad between Havana and Bejucal began on 9 October 1835.

With eight months to complete the most dangerous and experimental part of the works, a large and transient workforce was needed to drain the swampy ground along the route, excavate rocky terrain with explosives and build tunnels and embankments.[18] The Royal Development Council revived an earlier 'white colonisation' strategy devised by the Council for White Population (*Junta de Población Blanca*), responsible for promoting white immigration. The Railroad Commission applauded the plan to import up to two thousand labourers from the United States as 'not only good for the railroad', but in a more rhetorical flourish announced, 'it will serve as an experiment to increase the white population and would have far reaching and momentous consequences'.[19] Echoing the royal decree of 1820, when the Spanish Crown first allowed Catholics who were not Spanish subjects to migrate to Cuba, the Hispano-Cuban white colonisation plan recommended the 'urgent promotion' of Catholics from countries friendly to Spain. In a well-worn pro-slavery polemic a senior colonial administrator, Agustin Ferrety, proclaimed in 1826 that 'our slaves on this island, generally speaking, are infinitely happier than the wage workers of Europe, and especially the degraded masses of Irish Catholics'. Targeting this worthy and potentially prolific source, Ferrety assured the Spanish court that many would jump at the opportunity to emigrate, claiming that 'whole parishes (*parroquias enteras*) from Ireland would transport themselves to a country where they were assured an honourable living and could openly profess the religion of their forbearers'.[20] The promise of an 'honourable living' for poor Catholic immigrants in the Spanish Caribbean colony, however, was defined more by class and race than any religious solidarity, given the coercions embedded in the peculiar mix of wage-labour and slavery in Cuba. Unlike enslaved workers, 'free' workers belonged to no one, so their employers took little or no responsibility for their maintenance or well-being; they were paid seasonally and only for days worked, and were dispensed with when their labour was no longer needed. Moreover, they had few rights and no protection as migrant labourers in a country where they had no family or social networks and no knowledge of the language. This type of alienated cheap labour could be more easily subjected to a highly coercive work regime modelled on slavery and was therefore ideal for a society, such as Cuba, in transition to capitalism. The railroad would introduce a concentration of contract labour, larger than anything yet seen on the sugar plantations, and mediated as it was through the industrialising centres of North America. In the circulation of commodities and labour on the wider Atlantic trade networks Irish migrants had some experience of adapting to the wider contending forces of colonialism and industrialisation through harsh experiences of migration. In the trajectory from Ireland to Cuba they formed part of a small flow of European migrant labour in the nineteenth-century Spanish Caribbean within larger migratory flows of forced African labour, contract labour from the Canary Islands and later Chinese indentured labour.

By 1835, Irish emigrant workers had already established themselves as pioneering labour on the construction of the Baltimore and Ohio railroad and were some of the first European migrants to work on the Erie Canal, forming an army of brute labour 'who journeyed from job to job on public works'.[21] This transient way-of-life of the seasoned navvy was lived out in remote areas along the tracks and canals of early industrial America, often accompanied by their wives and children in shanty towns. The Chief Engineers on the Cuban railroad relied on immigrant networks on the canals and railroads of North America to recruit contractors who could mobilise a large force of semi-skilled and unskilled workers. With seasonal lay-offs in large construction works during the winter months, it was envisaged that migrant labourers would work from November to June, the dry season in Cuba, and return to the North on finishing their contracts. In an era of strong anti-Catholic sentiment Irish immigrants flocked to one of the first Catholic churches in New York ministered to by the exiled Cuban priest, Fr. Felix Varela, providing a ready nucleus of cheap labour easily lured by the promises of the contractors.

Los Irlandeses

In November 1835, the Spanish Consul signed contracts with captains of four ships – the *Havre, Roanoke, Choctaw* and *San Miguel* – to transport tools, equipment and workers for the Royal Development Council. The ships left New York early in November and after two to three weeks at sea they docked in Havana.[22] The collective term *los irlandeses* was given to the recruits from the United States, mostly of Irish origin, but there were also German, English, Scottish and American workers amongst them. In what was a predominantly male cohort, some women and children travelled with their husbands with one mother, Mrs. Campbell, accompanying her son John and one woman, Catherine McMahon, travelling independently. The American Consul, Nicholas Trist, commented '[...] not only men but entire families embracing women and children appear to have been attracted hither by offers of employment on the rail-road [...]'.[23] Estimates of the number of Irish workers who came to Cuba vary from five hundred to 'upwards of a thousand'. For the period November 1835 to November 1836, as the following table shows there were between 800 and 1,200 *irlandeses* out of a total of 2,749 labourers working on the section of railroad between Havana and Güines.

Number and category of railroad workers (1835–1836)

Origin of the Railroad Workers	
Capitanía General de Cuba	140 prisoners
Acueducto de Fernando VII	87 *emancipados* (freed slaves)
Real Junta de Fomento	145 slaves 200/250 cimarrones 927 *isleños* (Canary Islanders) 800/1,200 *irlandeses*
TOTAL	**2,299/2,749 labourers**

Source: Eduardo Moyano Bazzani, *La Nueva Frontera del Azucar: el Ferrocarril y La Economia Cubana del Siglo XIX*. (Madrid, 1991), p. 109

The surviving ships manifests in the records of the *Junta de Fomento* provide the names, surnames and occupations of three-hundred and sixty-four men described as artisans, carpenters or cartwrights, mechanics and overseers, but the majority were described as labourers. The Irish recruits were described as semi-skilled with experience in explosives and railroad construction.[24] Their contracts simply stated that the same conditions of work prevailing in the United States applied in Cuba. Monthly pay amounted to twenty-five pesos[25] but, as the contract states, 'the *Junta de Fomento* have to pay the cost of our passage to the owners of the ships and provisions for which we are in agreement that deductions of no more than thirteen pesos are made from our salary'.[26] Rudimentary accommodation was provided but food, clothes and medical attention were the workers' own responsibility. Pay was withheld for days not worked due to illness, bad weather or absenteeism.[27] Taking care to protect the interests of the investors, the engineers cautioned that these kinds of labourers who are generally 'poor and careless' could not be trusted to pay their debts. Judging by the number of chits contained in the records signed by Wright and Stoughton authorising 'advances on pay', many of the workers were indebted to the company before boarding the ships in New York. Workers were bound to the contractors until all outstanding debts were paid. The contracts were open-ended stating a term of six months to a year, as the *Junta de Fomento* wished (*a la voluntad de la Junta*). At the outset, in order to prevent loss of capital through desertions, the engineers secured an alliance between the colonial authorities, ship's captains and the contractors, to prevent the departure of imported workers until they had paid the cost of their transport to Cuba.

Soon after the arrival of the Irish the *Junta* signed agreements with shipping agents in the Canary Islands to import contract workers in good health, robust, hard-working and between the ages of twenty and forty. Referred to as *isleños,* the Spanish-speaking Canary Islanders were already present in Cuba in significant numbers with established social and family networks in the agricultural sector, growing tobacco and farming cattle. Historically their migration to Cuba was 'like indentured labourers to the British colonies of the past, contracted to work for a specific period but afterwards free'.[28] Mostly illiterate, rural workers from Tenerife with little experience of capitalist labour relations, they were no better equipped than the Irish recruits for the conditions of exploitation they would encounter.[29]

Conditions were grim, with a sixteen-hour working day of back breaking work and the well-being and survival of the workers depended on the contractors for their wages and supplies of food and clothing. It often happened that provisions fell short, resulting in workers having to exist on meagre food rations and without much needed medical attention. The coercions of debt-bondage, implicit in both the Irish and Canary Islander contracts, left few options: to stay on the job and hope to survive the extreme and brutal conditions, or risk incurring harsh punishments for protest or desertion. For some the dangers inherent in the railroad contracts made it a fatal choice, as the number of deaths testifies. Figures for Irish fatalities do not appear in the records consulted. In the case of the *isleños*, in what was more like a short-term indenture, repatriation on termination of the contracts was guaranteed. The terms and conditions of the Irish contracts, on the other hand, contained elements of the modernising influence of wage-labour. The contractors bought their services at a higher price than the Canary Islanders and bore no responsibility for their wellbeing or repatriation. These distinctions in the conditions of Irish and Canary Island labour demonstrate not only the articulation of processes of labour with migration but also the different experiences of labour relations between countries of origin and destination. Even though the harshness of day-to-day working conditions in a plantation economy was equally brutal for both groups of immigrants there were crucial differences between the Canary Island contracts and the Irish contracts that point to different trajectories of proletarianisation.

Hierarchies of Control

The mobilisation of such a large 'free' labour force presented new challenges to the colonial authorities in finding ways to exert control over the productivity and division of railroad labour. Despite conflicting ideologies on the superiority of free labour over slavery, capitalist managers voiced no moral qualms when it came to the enforcement of coercive labour practices in controlling this new category of European contract-labour. The colonial authorities, accustomed as they were to the management of plantation slavery, and the engineers with their experience of capitalist labour relations in the US, were united in their aim of profitably extracting labour while privileging the interests of those who purchased it. Cuba's sugar economy, dependent on slavery for its prosperity, relied on the colonial authorities to rigorously enforce a racial hierarchy typical of slave-based plantation societies. Kruger and the *Junta de Fomento* agreed on the imposition of a hierarchy of segregation and exclusion used to secure the boundaries of race and legal status amongst the railroad workforce. Segregation and control was structured in the built environment to accommodate workers and reinforced materially by a hierarchy of food rations.

In keeping with the social hierarchy of Cuba at the time, the large influx of foreign labourers was defined, demarcated and disciplined, based on a colonial imaginary of race, ethnicity and class. This is vividly spelt out in the engineers' conferral of privilege based on juridical status, which was conceived to segregate the workers as follows:

> [i]t will be necessary to specify distinctly in the contract the quantity and quality of food for the whites, whether hired labourers, prisoners or blacks, for which purpose it will be expedient to keep separate the different classes of labourers [...].

The differentiation of food supplies and the demarcation of labour based on race, and category of worker were linked, in Kruger's

scheme, to disciplinary processes in the abstraction of labour. He
elaborates further on the dangers of association:

> ... and if this reason did not exist, I would strongly recommend
> that each colour and class be kept separate, for the white man is
> debased when compelled to work with the black, and the latter
> by his intimate association with the former, loses the respect he
> would otherwise entertain for the whites generally and becomes
> more difficult to govern [...] the same remark might apply to
> the prisoners and hired men and there is still a stronger reason in
> the last instance that a guard will be necessary for the prisoners
> and if they work conjointly with hired labourers the facilities for
> their escape are increased or to counterbalance it a larger force
> of soldiers must be sustained to ensure a corresponding degree
> of security. Another reason also would urge this separation that
> prisoners invariably require a rigorous treatment to obtain from
> them even an indifferent day's work and this example would create
> a similar habit among the rest.[30]

The different categories of contract-workers, convicts, and *emancipados*
were all denied freedom of movement, confined to the camps under
a military-style regime. Kruger's authoritative views on the need to
preserve the status quo of racial and class division by means of differential
food rations and segregated disciplinary practices, paid lip-service to
the superiority of nominally free workers over slave labour, a strongly
symbolic gesture in the discourse of social relations in a slave society. But
what was really at stake in this careful management of racial and juridical
categories was a well-founded fear of contagion of a common sense of
injustice, spilling across colour lines and threatening the boundaries
of race and class. White contract labourers, awarded petty privilege on
paper at least, were undoubtedly at the top of this lowly labour hierarchy,
but even they were in danger of contagion by what Kruger saw as the

'indifference' of the imprisoned, while at the same time representing a risk of contagion by liberty (albeit limited) to the unfree. In other words discipline, control and spatial segregation on the tracks of the railroad not only implemented colonial policy in safeguarding the boundaries of race, equally such practices were designed to guard against the formation of horizontal relations and alliances across the ranks of a subaltern and multi-ethnic labour force.

Injury and mortality rates amongst the workforce were very high due to appalling work conditions and gruelling and dangerous, physical labour. Of course medical attention fell far short of what was promised, and as portrayed in Turnbull's account, 'as soon as anyone fell sick or was maimed, as many of them were in the service, they were instantly paid off and left to their own resources or beggary'.[31] During the rainy season in 1836, there were two reported outbreaks of cholera in the encampments along the railway tracks. Fear turned to panic as was common with such epidemics and workers began to riot or flee the encampments. An account of a cholera outbreak amongst Irish workers on the Chesapeake and Ohio canal in 1832 testifies that many Irish survived by fleeing north to Pennsylvania.[32] Military force was used in Cuba to quell riots and to prevent against desertions. Assessing the grim death toll, Moreno-Fraginals concludes that, just like sugar, the Güines railroad 'was made with blood'. There are no recorded deaths of Irish workers in the parish records of El Cerro or Bejucal, but Moreno-Fraginals estimates that 'there were as many Canary Island and Irish dead as there were blacks – perhaps more, for dead Canary Islanders and Irishmen represented no loss of invested capital'.[33]

Desertion and Destitution

In the management and control of labour in Cuba, physical force and brutality were permitted in the slave code to increase productivity. Contract workers were subjected to daily moral and physical degradation but as far as the records reveal, there is no evidence to suggest that they were subjected to the overseer's lash on a routine basis. In the management of 'free' workers the contractors used starvation and debt as leverage to coerce productivity and discipline. Incentives to productivity worked their way down a chain of command in a hierarchy of coercion. Penalties were imposed on contractors for delays in schedules agreed for different sections of the railway line, due to loss of labour through illness, worker insubordination or financial miscalculations. In turn the contractors who found themselves in debt to the company and unable to pay their workers or the suppliers of food often chose to flee the railroad. Bound by their contracts to the *Junta de Fomento*, angry labourers were forced to continue working under intolerable circumstances. Inevitably they protested, downing tools and demanding what was owed to them. The coercions of the contract and the threat of penal sanction ceased to compel a now desperate and angry mob to submit. Within weeks of their arrival violent riots broke out amongst the Irish, who armed themselves with knives and sticks. As early as 16 December 1835, rebellion by striking workers was dealt with by the full force of the military government. Cuban historian, Moreno-Fraginals argues that because the Irish and Canary Islanders represented almost a fifty-percent saving in labour costs, the company was prepared to go to any lengths to prevent them from leaving the job for better-paid work.[34] In a denial of the deception, intimidation and force used to control the labour force, the Chief Engineer, Kruger, invoked what Thomas Holt describes as the 'sanctified concept of the contract' emphasising the 'exercise of choice and the contractual nature of their service.'[35] There was no question of breach of contract, in Kruger's view, more a matter of dissatisfaction by the workers:

Those who are not satisfied with the terms of their contracts and wish to leave the service of this government, are at liberty to do so if they have paid all their debts in relation to their passage and accommodation, and they must leave the island within three days

[...] and [after three days] they will be treated with all the rigour
of the vagrancy laws of the country [...].

Maintaining the rhetoric of 'free' labour, Kruger, in a report to
the authorities, laid the blame for unrest and social disorder on
the ethnic shortcomings of the *irlandeses* imported from the
north:

> [...] however much the engineers need the services of those
> workers imported from the north, under no circumstances will they
> be allowed to work constantly in a drunken state, insubordinate
> and disobeying the overseers; neither will their requests for more
> pay be tolerated [...] anyone unhappy with their contracts can go
> back to the United States from where they came such a short time
> ago, and at their own expense.[36]

The system of contract, introduced by the engineers, was backed up
by the rule of law, through which immigrants were criminalised as
vagrants. Unlike the US, where Irish immigrants, as 'free white persons'
had an automatic 'presumption of liberty' and a right to become
citizens, their freedom in Cuba was inhibited to such an extent that any
attempt to escape debt-bondage quickly landed them in prison. Military
force was employed to attempt to control this audacious force of 'free'
labourers from the United States. The Railroad Commission provided
the authorities with a list of names of all the foreign workers, so that if
apprehended they could be returned immediately to the railroad; this
time without the ritual of contracts, as forced labour.[37] For their 'crimes'
those returned to the line had accumulated even greater debts with
the addition of penalties imposed for desertion and the cost of their
apprehension.

Some completed their contracts and were dispensed with by the *Junta de Fomento* without the means to leave the island and many ended up in the poorhouse or begging in the streets of Havana and in the countryside.[38] Foreign migrants died in jail or on the streets waiting in the vain hope of a passage out of Cuba. When the Captain-General Tacón proposed to house them 'in the prison of the *Cabañas* […] but although their suffering must have been extreme, not a single individual accepted the offer, preferring without exception, the precarious resource of eleemosynary aid'.[39] British Consul David Tolmé reported to the Foreign Office in London on his efforts to ease the hardship of British subjects as follows: 'On the whole I hope your lordship will think, viewing the immense influx of labourers of the lower classes, mostly Irish, who seldom thrive here that my expenditure on account of Government has been kept within the bounds of just economy'.[40] The *Junta de Fomento* washed its hands of any responsibility for those who became destitute having been, as they claimed, so well looked after during the time of their contracts:

> The foreigners brought from New York […] have no right in their contract (which they freely signed) to have the cost of their return paid by the Junta de Fomento. If they have finished their contract in the stipulated time or are fired and don't have the resources to pay their return or if they say they can't pay (something which can't be proved except by their own word) for this reason it is rare that the money will be provided out of the limited funds of public works.[41]

Only three months into the contracts, the American Consul dealt with petitions for aid from 'a number of unhappy workers, Americans, Irish and German' who became destitute. He wrote to the office of the Captain-General, Miguel Tacón: 'on the subject of certain Irishmen discharged from the work of the railroad one of whom has died and the rest are threatened with the same fate, owing to their present state of destitution and abandonment'. Another Englishman, George Webster, was thrown off the railroad declared to be suffering from 'mental derangement'. He was later arrested, ending up in prison with others from the railroad, guilty of wandering undocumented in the streets.[42] A letter written on behalf of a group of workers, in possession of documents to say they had paid their debts and were free to leave, pleaded with Tacón to put them on a boat back to where they came from, 'having worked so hard they are left with nothing to buy food or lodgings until they can find a boat to take them'.[43] The American Consul wrote to Tacón, saying:

> Scarcely a day passed without one or more of these miserable people presenting themselves to this consulate, which is no way authorised to afford relief to any class of persons […] Yesterday I sent off by the brig Sarah to New Orleans, a poor woman who with two young children had accompanied her husband from New York. She was utterly destitute; and to pay her debts to the people who had received her and her children in their house, and her passage to New Orleans I was obliged to advance out of my own pocket the sum of sixty dollars, not one *real* of which will ever be repaid to me.[44]

He berated the *Junta de Fomento* for allowing this 'class of person' to desert, as '[t]hey will fill the jails with navies [sic] whose only crime was to trust those who lured them to Cuba with promises they had no intentions of fulfilling'. Trist appealed to the Captain-General in February 1836 to do something about the situation, highlighting, 'the consequences which would inevitably arise from the want of some regulations whereby persons importing white labourers to be employed on the railroad should be required to provide against their becoming destitute vagabonds'.[45] The only possible remedy, as suggested by Trist was that the authorities should ensure that 'the persons charged with providing labourers for the railroad to be responsible for the transportation out of the island as every foreigner whom they may attract hither or take into their employ after his arrival here, as soon as such foreigners may be discharged from paid work or may leave it'.[46]

'Waged', 'White', but Not 'Free'

Irish railroad workers, intractable in their protest against such extreme coercion, drew on what Thompson argues is a 'lived experience' of resistance to processes of change and class formation which began in Ireland and continued to unfold in the radically different world of industrialising America. In this Caribbean colonial context, as newly proletarianised immigrants in a highly coercive system which valorised 'free' labour, Irish workers most likely drew on repertoires of resistance from the Irish countryside and adapted through the migrant's consciousness of freedom. From the perspective of slave-owning elites with a sense of ownership of labour power, the insubordinate workers posed a constant threat to the social order of the colony and to the emerging order of capitalist labour relations. Creole nationalists may have sympathised with the plight of British colonial subjects in Ireland, however, the economic imperatives of sugar production did not permit solidarity with immigrant labourers, who were co-religionists but not of their class. In the colonial order of things Irish labourers were closer to the status of enslaved African labour, and subjected as they were to the violence of coercive labour practices based on race and juridical status, the 'wages of whiteness' were meaningless in this context. The 'wage' did not confer status and even less so sufficient reward for one's labours, because materially, the so-called wage fell below what was necessary for social reproduction (arguably implicit in the idea of a wage). When it came to profits, the project of 'whitening' the nation paled in the hierarchy of concerns, uppermost in the minds of the sugar planting elites.

The earlier designation of Catholic *irlandeses* as a likely buffer against what was perceived as cultural contamination by the increased population of African labour, was quickly blemished by a 'disinclination to work' and as Stoler puts it, the characteristic 'indolence and insolence' of an inferior class.[47] As members of a white labouring class they were depicted by the *Junta de Fomento* as an exception to the rule of free market labour relations:

> They were our first exercise in increasing the white population [...] even though as "free labour" we exceeded their contracts, providing the necessities of their accommodation, increased their pay and provided assistance when they were sick; but the incredible drunkenness, of the majority of these miserable wretches [...] those who would abandon the job without permission end up roaming the countryside and towns, they are caught by police and brought back to their posts [...].

In their view the authorities simply erred in their choice of ethnicity in this free-labour experiment:

> [...] doubtless, as predicted by the American Consul, many of these will suffer and perish, no matter how they are treated or whatever country they are in; wherever else they bring their excesses they take the same risk of not being recompensed for their work.[48]

In June 1836 the *Junta de Fomento* defended its refusal to repatriate the Irish with a parting shot: 'those worthless, lazy, disease-ridden, drunkards deceived their bosses by disguising their vile habits at the time of their contracts [and] should have been thrown out much earlier'.[49] In contrast to the moral critique by the *Junta de Fomento*, a statement by the Railroad Commission suggests an economic motive for the rejection of Irish workers in favour of a new source of significantly cheaper labour from the Canary Islands:

> Henceforth they [Canary Islanders] could prove to be the most
> economic of workers, now that the company has liberated itself
> from the high daily wage paid to the Irish [...] despite the
> extraordinary attention necessary to manage them and the high
> cost of their labour – without them it would not have been possible
> to begin the railroad. It was a clever move to bring them here.[50]

The next experiment in cheap expendable workers, following the
example of the British West Indies, looked outside the continents of
Africa, Europe and the Americas to the most recent traffic in labour
from the Asian continent. Cuban planters enthusiastically embraced
a legal trade in Chinese indentured labour to supplement rather than
substitute slave labour. It cost as little as six hundred pesos to buy the
labour of a Chinese person contracted for eight years. In the aftermath
of the European contracts, and a hardening of attitudes towards the
substitution of slavery with 'free' labour, colonial elites, introduced
a clause to the Chinese contracts to 'renounce the exercise of all civil
rights' to 'assure their subordination and discipline'.[51]

Conclusion

The 'facts', as presented in the reportage of the colonial archives,
generate an image of Irish ethnicity as resistant to the modern state in
1830's Cuba, which displaces an earlier depiction of their potential as
whitening agents in the project of inventing a separate and white Cuban
nation. These documents also throw light on the discursive strategies of
the colonial elites underpinned by a logic of labour relations based on
the right to property in human beings. Protest and resistance by Irish
railroad workers disrupted the opaque logic of a transition from slavery
to free labour as articulated in colonial discourse. The contradictions
inherent in the rationale for importing cheap white labour as a likely
substitute for slavery were laid bare by the coercions remaining at the
heart of 'free' labour. The trajectory of these pre-famine Irish emigrants

to the Spanish colony of Cuba when analysed against the backdrop of a trans-colonial circuit of exploitation and control by capitalist enterprise demonstrates the formation of new and legal categories of unfree labour in an era of emancipation. Such discourses of race and labour shift according to, as Stoler terms it, the 'common sense' of colonial sense and reason, which 'conjoined social kinds with the political order of things' and that was subject to revision and actively changed.[52] In the reformulation of ethnicity, labour and coercion in the Cuban context, Irish migrants, no more than migrants from the African continent or the Canary Islands were far from passive instruments in the evolving order of labour relations and drew on their own accumulated experiences of adaptation and resistance to constraints which inhibited their freedom in ways they had not previously experienced.

ENDNOTES

1 PREFACE

1 See Nessa Cronin, Seán Crosson and John Eastlake (eds), *Anáil an Bhéil Bheo: Orality and Irish Culture* (Newcastle, 2009).

2 Some recent work in this area includes the following: Wanda Balzano, Ann Mulhall and Moynagh Sullivan (eds), *Irish Postmodernisms and Popular Culture* (Basingstoke, 2007); Martin McCloone, *Film, Media and Popular Culture in Ireland* (Dublin, 2008); Joe Cleary, *Outrageous Fortune: Capital and Culture in Modern Ireland* (Dublin, 2007); Eoin Flannery and Michael Griffin (eds), *Ireland in Focus* (New York, 2009); Mike Cronin and Roisín Higgins, *Places we Play: Ireland's Sporting Heritage* (Dublin, 2011).

3 *Irish Times*, 17 Feb. 2007.

2 RECYCLING IRISH POPULAR CULTURE

1 See Garreth Williams, 'Popular Culture and the Historians', in Peter Lambert and Phillipp Schofield (eds), *Making History: An Introduction to the History and Practices of a Discipline* (London and New York, 2004), pp. 257–68.

2 See James S. Donnelly and Kerby A. Miller (eds), *Irish Popular Culture, 1650–1850* (Dublin, 1998).

3 Donal O'Sullivan, 'Dublin Slang Songs, with Music', in *Dublin*

Historical Record, vol. 1, no. 3 (1938), 75–93.

4 James Kelly, *Gallows Speeches from Eighteenth-century Ireland* (Dublin, 2001); Niall Ó Ciosáin, *Print and Popular Culture in Ireland, 1750–1850* (Second ed., Dublin, 2010). To an extent, a similar argument could also be made in regards to more factual contemporary news reportage, which was examined in a study of crime in the period that mainly drew upon the *Hibernian Journal*; see Brian Henry, *Dublin Hanged: Crime, Law Enforcement and Punishment in late Eighteenth-century Dublin* (Dublin, 1994).

5 See Francis Grose, *A Classical Dictionary of the Vulgar Tongue* (London 1785); also Eric Partridge, *The Routledge Dictionary of Historical Slang* (London, 1973).

6 S.J. Connolly, *Divided Kingdom: Ireland, 1630–1800* (Oxford and New York, 2008), p. 337.

7 *Walker's Hibernian Magazine, or, Compendium of Entertaining Knowledge* (1787), Plate LXII.

8 *Young Squire Reynolds's Welcome Home to Ireland; to which are added, II. Larry's Ghost. III. De Night before Larry was Stretch'd* (Monaghan, 1788).

9 Andrew Carpenter, *Verse in English from Eighteenth-century Ireland* (Cork, 1998), p. 430.

10 See Seán Donnelly, 'A German Dulcimer Player in Eighteenth-century Dublin', in *Dublin Historical Record*, vol. 53, no. 1 (2000), 77–86.

11 Bodleian Library, Johnson Ballads 377; this broadside, printed in London and sold by J. Evans, no. 41, Long-Lane, is dated in the The English Short Title Catalogue to 1791–1803.

12 *The Festival of Anacreon: Containing a Collection of Modern Songs, written for the Anacreontic Society, the Beef-steak, and Humbug Clubs* (London, 1790; orig. ed. 1789), p. 23; *Paddy*

Whack's Bottle Companion; A Collection of Convivial Songs in High Estimation, many of which were Never Before Published (London, 1791), p. 49.

13 See *A Collection of above one Hundred and Fifty Choice Songs and Ballads* (Second ed., London, 1735), p. 173.

14 Cf.J.O. Bartley, 'The Development of a Stock Character: The Stage Irishman to 1800', in *The Modern Language Review*, vol. 37, no. 3 (1942), 438–47 (esp. 444–7).

15 *The Morning Post*, 21 Jan. 1789; cited in Simon McVeigh, *Concert Life in London from Mozart to Haydn* (Cambridge and New York, 1993), p. 11.

16 *Athenaeum*, no. 982 (22 Aug. 1846), pp. 862–3 [Thoms's letter is dated 12 Aug. and signed under the pseudonym Ambrose Merton].

17 McVeigh, *Concert Life in London*, pp. 8, 33–4, 83, 127.

18 *The Festival of Anacreon*, p. 3.

19 Letter to Alexander Pope, 30 Aug. 1716; *The Works of Dr Jonathan Swift* (8 vols., Edinburgh, 1757), iv, p. 19.

20 Richard Traubner, *Operetta: A Theatrical History* (Rev. ed., New York, 2003), pp. 10–11, 175.

21 J.C. Greene and G.L.H. Clark, *The Dublin Stage, 1720–1745: A Calendar of Plays, Entertainments, and Afterpieces* (Cranbury, NJ and London, 1993), p. 111.

22 Barra Boydell, 'Opera, 1660–1800' in W.J. McCormack (ed.), *The Blackwell Companion to Modern Irish Culture* (Oxford, UK and Malden, Mass., 1999), p. 447.

23 For an early example see the broadside *The Golden Harvest* (London, 1795).

24 *Lord Save us, the Congress are Fighting!* (Alexandria, D.C., 1798).

The song, one of several contemporary poetic satires on the violent clash between Republican congressman Matthew Lyon of Vermont and Federalist congressman Roger Griswold of Connecticut (30 Jan. and 15 Feb. 1798), comes out in support of Irish-born Lyon ('that honest old grey headed Pat…he's a sound hearted good democrat'). For the heavily-publicised scandal see James Fairfax McLaughlin, *Matthew Lyon, the Hampden of Congress, a Biography* (New York, 1900), pp. 225–304; Aleine Austin, *Matthew Lyon, 'New Man' of the Democratic Revolution, 1749–1822* (University Park and London, 1981), pp. 96–102.

25 Robert Bisset, *Douglas; or, the Highlander* (4 vols., London, 1800), iv, p. 196.

26 *Chapter of Admirals to which are added, The Night before Larry was Stretch'd, Tom Careless, The New Way of The Short Body'd Gown, Patrick O'Neal's Return fro[m] Drubbing the French, Anacreontic Song* (Glasgow, c. 1790); the broadside *The Night before Larry was Stretch'd* (Nottingham, *circa* 1798) also includes 'The Chapter of the Admirals'; Bodleian Library, Harding B 12 (158).

27 W.J. Fitzpatrick, *'The Sham Squire' and the Informers of 1798, with a View of their Contemporaries, to Which are Added Jottings about Ireland Seventy Years Ago* (Third ed., London and Dublin, 1866), pp. 50–1, 173–8.

28 See Kevin Whelan, 'The United Irishmen, the Enlightenment and Popular Culture', in David Dickson, Dáire Keogh and Kevin Whelan (eds), *The United Irishmen: Republicanism, Radicalism and Rebellion* (Dublin, 1993), pp. 269–96.

29 *The Irish Harp (Attun'd to Freedom): A Collection of Patriotic Songs; Selected for Paddy's Amusement* (Dublin, 1798), pp. 77–80.

30 *The Chapter of Kings, Sung by Mr. Collins, in his Brush* (London,

c. 1795).

31 See M.H. Thuente, 'United Irish Poetry and Songs' in J.M. Wright (ed.), *A Companion to Irish Literature* (2 vols., Chichester, 2010), ii, pp. 304–6.

32 T.C. Croker (ed.), *Memoirs of Joseph Holt, General of the Irish Rebels, in 1798* (2 vols., London, 1838), i, p. 311.

33 See Terry Moylan, *The Age of Revolution: 1776–1815 in the Irish Song Tradition* (Dublin, 2000), pp. 125–7.

34 *An excellent new copy of verses, called, by way of its title, De Sorrowful Lamentation of De Bowld Jemmy O'Brien, late keeper of bloody Bedford Tower, chief perjurer to De Battalion of testimony, spy, informer and assassin in Ordinary to De Orange tribunal, and first aid De Camp to Major Sirrevernce; who danced De Kilmainham Minuet at De Sheriff's swing swong, in Green-street, on Monday 21st July, 1800, for De Wanton, wilful, cruel, and cold-blooded murder, Mr. John Hoey, of Essex-street, in De Ospidal Fields, on Sunday the 4th day of May, 1800* (Dublin, 1800).

35 *Who's to Blame? A New Ballad on the Union* (Dublin, 1799), published by the Dublin bookseller Vincent Dowling at his Apollo Circulating Library, No. 5, College Green.

36 J.T. Gilbert, *A History of the City of Dublin* (Second ed., 3 vols., Dublin and London, 1861), iii, pp. 52–3; J.W. Ebsworth (ed.), *The Bagford Ballads: Illustrating the Last Years of the Stuarts* (2 vols., Hertford, 1878), ii, pp. 415–6. This ballad was reproduced on broadsides; see for example Bodleian Library, Harding B 25 (194) and B 11 (291).

37 Cf. Georges Denis Zimmerman, *Songs of Irish Rebellion: Irish Political Street Ballads and Rebel Songs, 1780–1900* (Second ed., Dublin, 2002).

38 See J.H. Murphy, *Ireland: A Social, Cultural and Literary History, 1791–1891* (Dublin, 2003), pp. 49–64.

39 See W.H.A. Williams, *Tourism, Landscape, and the Irish Character: British Travel Writers in Pre-Famine Ireland* (Madison, 2008), pp. 63–79.

40 S.M.T., 'Dublin, in 1822', in *New Monthly Magazine and Literary Journal*, 3 (1822), pp. 503–4.

41 *The Universal Songster; or, Museum of Mirth: Forming the Most Complete, Extensive, and Valuable Collection of Ancient and Modern Songs in the English Language* (3 vols., London, 1826), iii, pp. 140–1.

42 Weekes (ed.), *The Shamrock; A Collection of Irish Songs, Many of them Scarce, or Never Before Published but in a Separate State; With Several Originals* (Glasgow, Edinburgh and London, 1830), pp. v–ix. 'The Night before Larry was Stretched' is on pp. 109–11. A devastating review claimed that Weekes was 'perfectly ignorant of the subject' and that his collection mainly consisted of 'spurious trash'; see 'National Song of Ireland' in *Fraser's Magazine for Town and Country*, 3, no.17 (June, 1831), 537–56.

43 For a study of the wake see Gearóid Ó Crualaíoch, 'The "Merry Wake"', in James S. Donnelly, Jr., and Kerby A. Miller (eds), *Irish Popular Culture, 1650–1850* (Dublin, 1998), pp. 173–200.

44 C.M. Westmacott (ed.), *The Spirit of the Public Journals, for the year M.DCCC.XXV: Being an impartial selection of the most exquisite essays and jeux d'esprits, principally prose, that appear in the newspapers and other publications* (London, 1826), p. 345.

45 S.C. Hall, *Retrospect of a Long Life from 1815 to 1883* (New York, 1883), pp. 66–8; see also D.E. Latané, Jr., 'Charles Molloy Westmacott and the Spirit of the *Age*' in *Victorian Periodicals Review*, 40, no. 1 (2007), 44–72.

46 Bernard Blackmantle [C.M. Westmacott], *The English Spy: An original work, characteristic, satirical, and humorous; comprising scenes and sketches in every rank of society, being portraits of the illustrious, eminent, eccentric, and notorious* (Second ed., 2 vols., London, 1907), ii, pp. 22–33 (esp. p. 31).

47 *Fraser's Magazine for Town and Country*, 10 (1834), pp. 671–2.

48 F.S. Mahony, *The Reliques of Father Prout* (Third ed., London, 1860; revised and largely augmented), pp. 267–9. The book was repeatedly reissued in the nineteenth century, with editions coming out in 1836, 1860, 1866, 1870, 1876, 1881, and 1894.

49 Ibid., p. 140.

50 'The Rogueries of Tom Moore', ibid., pp. 131–59. See also Ethel Mannin, *Two Studies in Integrity: Gerald Griffin and the Rev. Francis Mahony ('Father Prout')* (London, 1954), pp. 135–262.

51 Reproduced in *Littell's Living Age*, Third ser., 9 (1860), p. 799. Mahony would be posthumously commended for the 'considerable power of language and of humour' in his translation of the ballad; see *Times of London*, 22 May 1866, p. 9.

52 T.C. Croker, *Popular Songs of Ireland* (London, 1839), xiv.

53 For a particularly harsh critique see B.G. MacCarthy, 'Thomas Crofton Croker 1798–1854' in *Studies*, vol. 32, no. 128 (1943), 539–56.

54 'The Ballad Poetry of Ireland', in *Monthly Chronicle*, vol. 3 (1839), 396, 398.

55 *Dublin University Magazine*, vol. 14, no. 79 (July 1839), 96–7. This implicitly nationalist review does not correspond to the general tone of the magazine, which was predominantly Protestant and Unionist. At least in the eyes of some, 'The Night Before Larry Was Stretched' was identified with Irish Protestant culture; see

Aodh de Blacam, 'The Other Hidden Ireland' in *Studies*, vol. 23, no. 91 (1934), 444.

56 J.E. Walsh, *Sketches of Ireland Sixty Years Ago* (Dublin, London and Edinburgh, 1847), pp. 82–6. New editions of this book came out in 1849, 1851 and 1859; the title was subsequently revised and updated to *Ireland Ninety Years Ago* (Dublin, 1876); *Ireland One Hundred and Twenty Years Ago* (Dublin and Waterford, 1911); *Rakes and Ruffians: The Underworld of Georgian Dublin* (Dublin, 1979).

57 Ibid., pp. iii–v.

58 Diary entry for 19 March 1842; J.R. Russell (ed.), *Memoirs, Journal, and Correspondence of Thomas Moore* (8 vols., London and Boston, 1853–6), vii, pp. 314–5.

59 W.H. Dixon (eds), *Lady Morgan's Memoirs: Autobiography, Diaries and Correspondence* (2 vols., London, 1862), ii, p. 543.

60 A.P. Graves, *Songs of Irish Wit and Humour* (London, 1884). Although Burrowes denied authorship of the song, he was known in Cork by the nickname 'Larry' in consequence of this attribution; see *Notes and Queries*, Fifth ser., 11 (5 Apr. 1879), 277.

61 'Revelations of Ireland' in *Dublin University Magazine*, 31, no. 181 (Jan. 1848), 3. This suggestion may derive from a misreading of a tradition, which attributed to Lysaght a satirical song from 1789 set to the tune of 'The Night before Larry was Stretched' (though not the original ballad); see Fitzpatrick, *The Sham Squire*, p. 174.

62 Frank O'Connor, *A Short History of Irish Literature: A Backward Look* (Second ed., New York, 1968), p. 128.

63 Walsh, *Sketches of Ireland*, pp. 84–5.

64 'Irish Street Songs' in *All the Year Round*, vol. 3, no. 78 (May, 1870), 620.

65 H.H. Sparling (ed.), *Irish Minstrelsy: Being a Selection of Irish Songs, Lyrics, and Ballads* (Second ed., London and New York, 1888; orig. ed. 1887), p. 514.

66 J.S. Farmer, *Musa Pedestris: Three Centuries of Canting Songs and Slang Rhymes [1536–1896]* (London, 1896), pp. 79–81, 220.

67 Stopford A. Brooke and T.W. Rolleston (eds), *A Treasury of Irish Poetry in the English Tongue* (New York and London, 1900), p. 8.

68 A.M. Williams, *The Poets and Poetry of Ireland: With Historical and Critical Essays and Notes* (Boston, 1881), pp.142–3.

69 For example, in the second half of the nineteenth century it appeared alongside eleven other songs on a broadside probably printed in Dublin by Nugent, J.F. and Co. and appeared on a broadside printed and sold at No. 16, Circus-street, Liverpool; Bodleian Library, Harding B 40(18) and B 28(199).

70 M.J. Barry (ed.), *The Songs of Ireland* (Dublin, 1845), pp. 208–9; additional Irish editions were published in 1846, 1847, 1849, 1857, 1860, 1869, 1874 (as well as a New York edition in 1873).

71 First published under the pseudonym Morty Macnamara Mulligan in *Blackwood's Edinburgh Magazine*, vol. 10, no. 59 (Dec. 1821), 613–7; republished in Croker, *Popular Songs of Ireland*, pp. 27–30.

72 National Library of Scotland. Elsewhere, An Irish Poet's Box was operated by James Moore in Belfast from 1846 to 1856.

73 M.A. Titmarsh [William Makepeace Thackeray], 'A Box of Novels', in *Fraser's Magazine for Town and Country*, 29, no. 170 (Feb., 1834), 154

74 Lady Morgan [Sydney Owenson], 'Memoirs of the Macaw of a Lady of Quality' in *The Mirror of Literature Amusement and Instruction*, 17 (1831), 333; see also *The Metropolitan*, 1 (1831), 38.

75 Samuel Lover, *Handy Andy: A Tale of Irish life* (London, 1842), p. 293.

76 C.J. Lever, *Jack Hinton, the Guardsman* (Dublin, 1843), pp. 18 and 116. References to songs set to the air also appear in C.J. Lever, *Tom Burke of 'Ours'* (Dublin, 1844), vol. 1, p. 80; C.J. Lever, *The Fortunes of Glencore* (London, 1857), vol. 1, pp. 37–8.

77 William Carleton, 'An Irish Election in the Time of the Forties', in *Dublin University Magazine*, 30 (Sept. 1847), 296.

78 Dion Boucicault, *The Colleen Bawn; or, the Brides of Garryowen: A Domestic Drama in Three Acts* (New York, 1860), p. 27.

79 J.M. Synge, *The Tinker's Wedding, A Comedy in Two Acts* (Dublin, 1907), pp. 12–3 and 24.

80 Nicholas Grene, 'Synge in Performance', in P.J. Mathews (ed.), *The Cambridge Companion to J.M. Synge* (Cambridge and New York, 2009), p. 156.

81 See M.P. Worthington, 'Irish Folk Songs in Joyce's Ulysses' in *PMLA*, 71, no. 3 (1956), 321–39.

82 James Joyce, *Ulysses* (New York, 1992; Modern Library ed.), p. 301.

83 Oliver St John Gogarty, *Mad Grandeur, A Novel* (Philadelphia and New York, 1941), chapter 3, pp. 330-341.

84 See Liam Miller, *The Dun Emer Press, later the Cuala Press* (Dublin, 1973), pp. 52 and 94; Gifford Lewis, "'The Terrible Struggle with want of Means": Behind the scenes at the Cuala Press', in Clare Hutton and Patrick Walsh (eds), *The Oxford History of the Irish Book, v: The Irish Book in English, 1891–2000* (Oxford, 2011), pp. 539–40. A digital version, courtesy of Villanova University Library, is available at http://digital.library.villanova.edu/ Cuala Press Broadside Collection/ Broadside-00045.xml (accessed 18 Dec. 2011).

85 See Eugene Mason, 'Mr. Jack B. Yeats and the Poets of "A Broadside"' in idem, *Considered Writers, Old and New* (London, 1925), pp. 225–31; originally published in *To-Day*, vol. 2, no. 8 (1917), 53–8.

86 Hector McDonnell, *The Night before Larry was Stretched* (Belfast, 1984). See also *Linen Hall Review*, vol. 2, no. 3 (Autumn, 1985), 11. When put up for sale at Whyte's Irish Art Auction in Dublin on 18 February 2003, copy no. 94 was sold for €150 (Lot 248).

87 *Colm Ó Lochlainn's More Irish Street Ballads* (Second ed., Dublin, 1968), pp. 235–7.

88 Frank Harte, *Dublin Street Songs* (Topic Records, 1967; reissued on CD in 2004).

89 Sleeve notes, Christy Moore, *The Iron Behind the Velvet* (Tara, 2002); see also repeated references posted on Christy Moore's official website: http://www.christymoore.com (accessed 21 Dec. 2011).

90 Wolfe Tones, *Irish to the Core* (Triskel Records, 1976; reissued on CD: Shanachie, 1993).

91 *Common Ground* (EMI Premier, 1996; produced by Dónal Lunny).

92 'O'Donoghue's Opera' (1965; dir. Kevin Sheldon; re-edited by Sé Merry Doyle, RTÉ); *Irish Times*, 2 Feb. 1998, p. 47. My thanks to Ms. Sheilah Harris, cultural attaché at the Irish Embassy in Israel for arranging for me to view the film.

93 For a recent example see Patrick Crotty (ed.), *The Penguin Book of Irish Poetry* (London, 2010), pp. 422–4.

94 See Matthew Gelbart, *The Invention of 'Folk Music' and 'Art Music': Emerging Categories from Ossian to Wagner* (Cambridge and New York, 2007).

95 P.V. Bohlman, *The Study of Folk Music in the Modern World* (Bloomington, 1988), p. 33.

96 See David Harker, *Fakesong: The Manufacture of British 'Folksong' 1700 to the Present Day* (Milton Keynes, 1985) and Georgina Boyes, *The Imagined Village: Culture, Ideology, and the English Folk Revival* (Manchester, 1993). For a critique see David Gregory, 'Fakesong in an Imagined Village? A Critique of the Harker-Boyes Thesis', in *Canadian Folk Music*, vol. 43, no. 3 (2011), 18–26.

3 'WE WERE SO DIFFERENT!': NEGOTIATING GENDER ON THE SHOWBAND STAGE

1 The author wishes to thank Tes Slominski for her thoughtful comments on early versions of this paper.

2 Mildred Beirne, interview, 17 July 2007.

3 Ibid.

4 Diarmaid Ferriter, *The Transformation of Ireland, 1900–2000* (London, 2005), p. 496, see also pp. 327–328.

5 Beirne, 2007.

6 Albert Reynolds, interview, 10 July 2006.

7 Gerry O'Hanlon, 'Population Change in the 1950s: A Statistical Review', in Dermot Keogh, Finbarr O' Shea and Carmel Quinlan (eds.), *The Lost Decade: Ireland in the 1950s* (Cork, 2004), p. 75.

8 Ferriter, *Transformation*, p. 463.

9 Tom Garvin, *Preventing the Future: Why was Ireland so Poor for so Long?* (Dublin, 2004), p. 105.

10 Ibid., p. 115.

11 G.J. Barker-Benfield, *The Culture of Sensibility: Sex and Society in 18th Century Britain* (Chicago, 1992), xxiv.

12 Sherrie Tucker, *Swing Shift: 'All-Girl' Bands of the 1940s* (Durham, N.C., 2000), p. 2.

13 Sandy Kelly, interview, 12 July 2008.

14 Tina Tully, interview, 14 July 2008.

15 Tucker, *Swing Shift*, p. 18.

16 Caitríona Clear, 'Too Fond of Going': Female Emigration and Change for Women in Ireland, 1946–1961', in *Ireland in the 1950s* (Cork, 2004), pp. 136, 145.

17 Eileen Kelly, interview, 8 July 2008.

18 Muriel Day, interview, 18 June 2008.

19 Ibid.

20 Tully, 2008.

21 Maxi McCoubrey, interview, 3 June 2009.

22 Kelley replaced well-known showband singer, Maisie McDaniels, who eventually went on to perform with the Fendermen.

23 Eileen Kelly, 2008.

24 Ibid.

25 Ibid.

26 Margo O'Donnell, interview, 17 July 2008.

27 Eileen Kelly, 2008.

28 Reid, as quoted in Vincent Power, *Send 'Em Home Sweatin': The Showbands' Story* (Dublin, 1990), p. 326.

29 O'Donnell, 2008.

30 Ibid.

31 Sandy Kelly, 2008.

32 Reid, as quoted in Power, *Send 'Em Home Sweatin'*, p. 333.

33 Philomena Begley, interview, 17 July 2008.

34 McCoubrey, 2009.

35 Day, 2009.

36 Eileen Kelly, 2008.

37 Beirne, 2006.

38 Day, 2009.

39 O'Donnell, 2008.

40 Helen Davis, 'All Rock and Roll is Homosocial: The Representation of Women in the British Rock Music Press', *Popular Music*, vol. 20, no. 3, *Gender and Sexuality* (2001), 301–302.

41 'Why Eileen Never Married (But Says Yes to New Band)', in *Dancing Gazette*, Dublin, Dec. 1966.

42 Eileen Kelly, 2008.

43 Susan McClary, *Feminine Endings: Music, Gender, and Sexuality* (Minneapolis, 1991), pp. 20–21.

44 'Why Eileen Never Married (But She Says Yes to New Band)', in *Dancing Gazette*, Dublin.

45 It is well worth noting here the huge variety in terms of marital status among women showband artists. Some chose not to marry nor have children, while others did marry. Some had children and retired from the stage, while others raised families (Philomena Begley, Sandy Kelly, Mildred Beirne, Eileen Reid and others) and maintained a life of performance, successfully finding a way to balance work and child rearing.

46 Eileen Kelly, 2008.

47 Ibid.

48 Annie Randall, *Dusty!: Queen of the Postmods* (Cary, NC, 2008), p. 71.

49 Rebecca Miller, "Our Own Little Isle': Irish traditional music in New York', *New York Folklore*, vol. xiv, nos. 3-4 (1988), 101–115.

50 Rebecca S. Miller, 'Irish Traditional and Popular Music in New York City: Identity and Social Change, 1930-1975', in R.H. Bayor and T.J. Meagher (eds), *The New York Irish: Essays Towards a History* (Baltimore, 1996), pp. 481-507.

51 Bill Malone, *Flowers in the Wildwood: Women in Early Country Music, 1923–1939*, notes to the CD (Munich, 2003), p. 13.

52 Historically, women Nashville artists spanned a range of stereotypes from the hayseed rube who dressed in gingham (Minnie Pearl, Lulu Belle in the 1930s) to the 1940s and 1950s cowgirl (Patsy Montana, Rose Maddox, for example) to Patsy Cline's look of modern sophistication in the late 1950s and 1960s, and to the hyper-femininity of Dolly Parton beginning in the 1960s. For more on imagery and female country artists, see Mary Bufwack, 'Girls with Guitars – And Fringe and Sequins and Rhinestones, Silk, Leather and Lace', in Cecilia Tichi (ed.), *Reading Country Music* (Durham, 1998), pp. 153–187.

53 Along with Big Tom, Philomena Begley and others, Margo O'Donnell's preference for the country style eventually contributed in the mid-1960s to the birth of a new genre, Country and Irish. This style combines country musical style with the vocal and lyrical elements of Irish folk song.

54 Sandy Kelly, 2008.

55 Ibid.

56 O'Donnell, 2008.

57 Ibid.

58 Ibid.

59 Anne McClintock, *Imperial Leather: Race, Gender and Sexuality in the Colonial Contest* (New York, 1995), pp. 358–9.

60 Begley, 2008.

61 Beirne, 2007.

62 Christina Baade, 'The Battle of the Saxes: Gender, Dancebands and British Nationalism in the Second World War', in Nichole T. Rustin and Sherrie Tucker (eds), *Big Ears: Listening for Gender in Jazz Studies* (Durham, N.C., 2008), p. 117.

63 Beirne, 2007.

64 Ibid.

4 SEÁN BURKE, LION OF LAHINCH: AN IRA MAN AT THE WALKER CUP

1 *Belfast Telegraph*, 4 June 2002.

2 William A. Menton, *The Golfing Union of Ireland 1891–1991* (Dublin, 1991), p. 227; see also Ivan Morris, *Only Golf Spoken Here: Colourful Memoirs of a Passionate Irish Golfer* (Chelsea MI, 2001), p. 187.

3 *Clare Champion*, 13 Aug. 1932.

4 See Menton, *The Golfing Union*, pp. 226–7; also p. 384.

5 John Lowerson, 'Golf', in Tony Mason (ed.), *Sport in Britain: A Social History* (Cambridge, 1989), pp. 187–214, p. 189.

6 See, for example, John Burnett, *Riot, Revelry and Rout: Sport in Lowland Scotland Before 1860* (Lothian, 2000), pp. 66–76; Richard Holt, *Sport and the British: A Modern History* (Oxford, 1989), pp. 71–2.

7 Holt, *Sport and the British*, p. 71.

8 See www.lahinchgolf.com [accessed: 26 Oct. 2012].

9 Daniel Mulhall, '"A Gift from Scotland": Golf's Early Days in Ireland', *History Ireland*, vol. 14, no. 5 (Sept./Oct. 2006), 34

10 Ibid.

11 Holt, *Sport and the British*, p. 133.

12 See Patrick Maume, 'Nationalist Attitudes to Golf', letter to *History Ireland*, vol. 15, no. 1 (Jan./Feb. 2007), 11.

13 For a comparative perspective, see Holt, *Sport and the British*, passim.

14 I am grateful to Patrick Burke, nephew of John Burke, for this and other information cited in this article.

15 See www.limerickgolfclub.ie/IvanMorris/LL69.pdf [accessed: 26 Oct. 2012].

16 'Editorial', *The American Golfer*, vol. 35, no. 8 (May, 1932), 11.

17 *Clare Champion*, 13 Aug. 1932.

18 See www.irishgolfarchive.com/Bio/ECarter.htm [accessed: 12 Oct. 2012].

19 See Patrick Lynch, 'A Fighting Rearguard Action Saved IRA in the Retreat after the Battle of Rineen', in *With the IRA in the Fight for Freedom: 1919 to the Truce* (Tralee, 1950), pp. 67–77, esp. p. 69; Burke is also mentioned in Ernie O'Malley's account of Rineen in Ernie O'Malley, *Raids and Rallies* (Dublin, 1982), pp. 67–90, p. 74.

20 See Michael Hopkinson, *The Irish War of Independence* (Dublin, 2002), p. 130.

21 Morris, *Only Golf*, p. 186.

22 Ibid.

23 The *Irish Times*, 1 Sept. 1932, and Menton, *The Golfing Union*, pp. 218–49. In an example of the ambiguity surrounding who was 'Irish', Menton does not include Brownlow in his list of Irish Walker Cup players.

24 *The Times*, 6 April 1932.

25 Quoted in Grantland Rice, 'Lining Up For the Walker Cup', *The American Golfer*, vol. 35, no. 11 (Aug., 1932), 24-5, 40.

26 *Clare Champion*, 16 April 1932.

27 *Clare Champion*, 13 Aug. 1932.

28 Quoted in *Clare Champion*, 23 April 1932.

29 *Irish Times*, 31 Aug. 1932.

30 For the story of Ouimet, Vardon and the 1913 US Open see Mark Frost, *The Greatest Game Ever Played: Vardon, Ouimet and the Birth of Modern Golf* (London, 2002).

31 *Clare Champion*, 10 Sept. 1932; Menton, *The Golfing Union*, p. 228.

32 Bernard Darwin, 'Echoes from Brookline', *The American Golfer*, vol. 36, no. 2 (Nov., 1932), 24, 41.

33 Morris, *Only Golf*, p. 186.

34 Ibid.

35 *The Times*, 1 Sept. 1932.

36 See Gordon G. Simmonds, *The Walker Cup, 1922-99: Golf's Finest Contest* (Droitwich, 2000).

37 Morris, *Only Golf*, p. 186.

38 *The Times*, 15 Aug. 1932.

39 Ibid.

40 *The Times*, 1 May 1934.

41 See www.irishgolfarchive.com/Bio/ECarter.htm [accessed: 12 Oct. 2012].

42 *The Times*, passim.

43 Menton, *The Golfing Union*, p. 226.

44 Burke was not the only Irish international golfer at this time with an IRA background. As Mark Wehrly has pointed out, John Graham – a prominent member of the IRA Northern Command

during the 1930s and 1940s, and a member of a 'special unit' comprised largely of Protestant IRA members – played with Burke on the Irish international team in 1938. See Wehrly, 'John S.S. Graham – international golfer and IRA commander, 1938-1951', at http://markwehrly.wordpress.com/golf-and-republicanism-in-the-1950s [accessed 10 Nov. 2011].

45 Quoted in *Belfast Telegraph*, 4 June 2002.

5 CORNER BOYS IN SMALL TOWN IRELAND, 1922–1970

1 James Joyce, *Dubliners* (Oxford, 2000).

2 Cited in David M. Doyle, *Sexual Crime and the Formulation of the Criminal Law Amendment Act 1935: A Quantitative, Historical and Legislative Analysis* (PhD thesis, National University of Ireland, Galway, 2010), p. 283.

3 Kathleen Kirwan, *Towards Irish Nationalism* (Dublin, 1938).

4 Stanley Van der Ziel (ed.), *John McGahern, Love of the World: Essays* (London, 2009), p. 97.

5 Ibid.

6 Anthony Cronin, *Dead as Dornails* (Swords, 1980), p. 4.

7 Glenn Jordan and Chris Weedon, 'Literature into Culture: Cultural Studies after Leavis', in Patricia Waugh (ed.), *Literary Theory and Criticism: An Oxford Guide* (Oxford, 2006), p. 247.

8 Terence Patrick Dolan (ed.), *A Dictionary of Hiberno-English: The Irish Use of English* (Dublin, 2004).

9 Geoffrey Pearson, *Hooligan: A History of Respectable Fears* (New York, 1983), pp. 74–79.

10 Personal Communication, Louis de Paor, 2010.

11 *The Times*, 19 Dec. 1891.

12 *Irish Times,* 7 Dec. 1996. On the order of business in the Dáil, Tánáiste Dick Spring withdrew his remark calling the Fíanna Fáil party 'chancers'. Attached – by whom it is not clear – to the notice circulated about the withdrawal was the page from the official rules on forbidden words, which contain the word *chancer.* Other banned words include liar, brat, buffoon, communist, corner boy, fascist, guttersnipe, hypocrite and rat. It is also forbidden to insinuate a member is drunk or disorderly.

13 *Sunday Independent*, 18 Nov. 2007.

14 Luke Gibbons, *Transformations in Irish Culture* (Cork, 1996), p. 163, citing G.J. Watson, *Irish Identity and the Literary Revival* (London, 1979), p. 28.

15 *Irish Times,* letters to the editor, G.J. Costello, 15 Sept. 1981, citing *Irish Times,* 18 July 1977.

16 *Irish Independent,* 10 March 1982.

17 *The Times,* 2 Nov. 1881.

18 *The Times,* 4 April 1939, 29 Dec. 1952, 29 Aug. 1955, 13 Dec. 1960, 19 May 1965, 18 Sept. 1967 and 23 March 1970.

19 J.A. Cuddon, *Penguin Dictionary of Literary Terms and Literary Theory* (Fourth edition., London, 1999), p. 165.

20 *Irish Times,* 19 May 1975.

21 Ibid.

22 William Desmond, *Being Between: Conditions of Irish Thought* (Galway, 2008), pp. 10–12. 'Metaxology: it weds the Greek '*metaxu*' the 'between' with the Greek '*logos*' meaning 'word'.

23 Charles Baudelaire, 'A Úne Passante', in Wm. J. Thompson, *Les Fleur du Mal: Critical Readings* (London, 1997), p. 158–9.

24 Walter Benjamin, *Illuminations* (London, 1992), pp. 168–9. The Berlin street corner boy, so called, was an actual person – an

eckensteher called Ferdinand 'Nante" Stumpf and was used as a character by a satirical writer, Adolf Glassbrenner, to score political points. Marx was a contemporary and would have been in Berlin around the same time, see Robert Justin Goldstein, *The War for the Public Mind: Political Censorship in Nineteenth-Century Europe* (Connecticut, 2000), p. 45.

25 *Leitrim Observer,* 29 Nov. 1995.

26 H.D.F. Kitto, *Greek Tragedy* (London, 1997), p. 159.

27 Patrick Kavanagh, 'Epic', *Selected Poems* (London, 1996), p. 102.

28 Robert A. Kaster (ed.), *Cicero: Speech on Behalf of Publius Sestius* (Oxford, 2006), pp. 34–5.

29 http://higherintellect.info/texts/thought_and_writing/ philosophy/Russell,%20Bertrand/Russell,%20Bertrand%20-%20 Collection%201.pdf, [accessed 5 Jan. 2012]. Emphasis added.

30 Edward V. Hong and Edna H. Hong (eds), *Kierkegaard's Writings, vol.7, Johannes Climacus, Philosophical Fragments, IV 176,* (Princeton, 1987), p. 6.

31 Giles Constable, 'Religious Communities, 1024–1215', in David Luscombe and Jonathan Riley Smith (eds),*The New Cambridge Medieval History, c.1024 – c.1198* (Cambridge, 2004), pp. 335–367, p. 354.

32 Gayatri Chakravorty Spivak, 'Marxism and the Interpretation of Culture', in Patrick Williams and Laura Chrisman (eds), *Colonial Discourse and Post-Colonial Theory: A Reader* (London, 1993), pp. 66–111.

33 Michel Foucault, *Discipline and Punish: The Birth of the Prison* (London, 1991), p. 216.

34 Ibid., p. 214.

35 Ibid., p. 210.

36 Ibid., p. 212.

37 Foucault, *Discipline and Punish: The Birth of the Prison* (London, 1991), pp. 201–2.

38 Foucault, *The Will to Power: The History of Sexuality, vol. 1* (Penguin, 1978), p. 11.

6 RETHINKING RURAL/URBAN: TRADITIONAL MUSIC AND MUSICAL COMMUNITY IN 21ST CENTURY DUBLIN

1 Helen O'Shea, *The Making of Irish Traditional Music* (Cork, 2008).

2 Jos. Koning, 'The Fieldworker as Performer: Fieldwork Objectives and Social Roles in County Clare, Ireland', *Ethnomusicology*, xxiv, no. 3 (1980), 417–429; Tony C. Kearns and Barry Taylor, *A Touchstone for the Tradition: The Willie Clancy Summer School* (Dingle, 2003).

3 See for example Deirdre Ní Chonghaile, '"Ag Teacht le Cuan": Irish Traditional Music and the Aran Islands' (PhD thesis, University College Cork, Cork, 2011); Sean Corcoran, 'Concepts of Regionalism in Irish Traditional Music' in Thérèse Smith and Mícheál Ó Súilleabháin (eds), *Blas: The Local Accent in Irish Music* (Limerick, 1995); Lillis Ó Laoire and Éamonn Mac Ruairí, *On a Rock in the Middle of the Ocean: Songs and Singers in Tory Island, Ireland* (Toronto, 2005); Niall Keegan, 'The Verbal Context of Style in Irish Traditional Music', in Thérèse Smith and Mícheál Ó Súilleabháin (eds), *Blas: The Local Accent in Irish Music* (Limerick, 1995); Frances Morton, 'Performing Ethnography: Irish Traditional Music Sessions and New Methodological Spaces', in *Social & Cultural Geography*, vi, no. 5 (2005), 661–676.

4 Fintan Vallely, *Tuned Out: Traditional Music and Identity in Northern Ireland* (Cork, 2008); Gary Hastings, *With Fife and Drum: Music, Memories, and Customs of an Irish Tradition* (Belfast, 2003).

5 O'Shea, *The Making of Irish Traditional Music*, p. 136.

6 Richard Kearney, *Postnationalist Ireland: Politics, Culture, Philosophy* (London, 1997), p. 63.

7 Adelaida Reyes Schramm, 'Explorations in Urban Ethnomusicology: Hard Lessons from the Spectacularly Ordinary', *Yearbook for Traditional Music*, xiv (1982), 1-14.

8 Ibid., p. 10.

9 For example, David Coplan, 'The Urbanisation of African Music: Some Theoretical Observations', *Popular Music*, ii (1982), 113–129.

10 Ruth Finnegan, *The Hidden Musicians: Music-making in an English Town* (Cambridge, 1989).

11 Ibid., p. 299.

12 Benedict Anderson, *Imagined Communities: Reflections on the Origin and Spread of Nationalism* (London, 1991).

13 Thomas Turino, *Nationalists, Cosmopolitans, and Popular Music in Zimbabwe* (Chicago, 2000), p. 48.

14 Andrew MacLaran, *Dublin: The Shaping of a Capital* (London, 1993), p. 148.

15 All descriptions of the Cobblestone and environs are based upon fieldwork conducted from 2007–2010.

16 David Farley, 'Changing Smithfield Still Holds on to Dublin-style Fun', in *New York Times* (23 Apr. 2009), sec. travel (http://travel.nytimes.com/2009/04/26/travel/26surfacing.html).

17 Turino, *Nationalists, Cosmopolitans, and Popular Music in Zimbabwe*, pp. 7–8.

18 Michel de Certeau, *The Practice of Everyday Life* (Berkeley and Los Angeles, 1988), p. 104. Gerry Smyth, *Space and the Irish Cultural Imagination* (New York, 2001), p. 84.

19 Mick O'Connor, 'History of the Piper's Club', in *Comhaltas Blog*, 2007 (http://comhaltas.ie/blog/post/history_of_the_pipers_club/).

20 Gay McKeon, interview, 29 June 2010.

21 Pat White, interview, 23 Jan. 1962 (Irish Traditional Music Archives, RTÉ Field Recordings, 1185-RTE-RR).

22 Aoife O'Brien, interview, 14 June 2010.

23 Aradhana Sharma and Akhil Gupta, *The Anthropology of the State: A Reader* (Oxford, 2006).

24 Toby Miller and George Yudice, *Cultural Policy* (London, 2002).

25 Judith Butler, *Gender Trouble: Feminism and the Subversion of Identity* (New York & London, 1990).

26 Gregory Barz, '"We are from Different Ethnic Groups but we Live Here as One Family": The Musical Performance of Community in Tanzanian Kwaya', in Karen Ahlquist (ed.), *Chorus and Community* (Urbana and Chicago, 2006), p. 26.

27 Michael Herzfeld, *Cultural Intimacy: Social Poetics in the Nation-State* (New York & London, 1997), p. 64.

28 Doreen B. Massey, *Space, Place, and Gender* (Minnesota, 1994), p. 8.

29 Paddy Glackin, interview, 15 June 2010.

7 THE RIDDLE OF RAVENHILL: THE 1954 IRISH RUGBY INTERNATIONAL IN BELFAST

1 *The Guardian*, 22 Aug. 2006.

2 For an overview of the political implications of Irish rugby, see Liam O'Callaghan, *Rugby in Munster – A Social and Cultural History* (Cork, 2011), Chapter 5.

3 Jason Tuck, 'Making Sense of Emerald Commotion: Rugby Union, National Identity and Ireland, in *Identities: Global Studies in Culture and Power*, vol. 10, no. 4 (2003), pp. 495–515.

4 Sean Diffley, *The Men in Green* (London, 1973), pp. 48–49.

5 *Irish Independent*, 11 Dec. 1973.

6 *Irish Press*, 21 March 1963.

7 Edmund Van Esbeck, *Irish Rugby 1874–1999* (Dublin, 1999), p. 101.

8 When contacted, the IRFU said it was unable to provide contacts with the surviving players because no records were kept. Later the IRFU failed to reply to both a letter and an email seeking information about the affair.

9 Letter from Ronnie Kavanagh to Vic Rigby, 19 April 2004.

10 For an overview see O'Callaghan, *Rugby in Munster*, Chapter 1.

11 For a full discussion, see Liam O'Callaghan, 'Rugby Football and Identity Politics in Free State Ireland', *Eire Ireland*, vol. 42, nos. 1-2 (forthcoming, 2013).

12 There were, of course, several Catholic officials but the Union's most powerful position, that of president, was dominated by Protestants until after the Second World War. See Ibid.

13 Daly to Jeffares, 2 Feb. 1932. Irish Rugby Football Union Papers, Miscellaneous Letters.

14 See O'Callaghan, *Rugby in Munster*, pp.170–175.

15 *Connacht Tribune*, 6 Feb. 1932.

16 See L.K. Donohue, 'Regulating Northern Ireland: The Special Powers Acts, 1922-1972', *The Historical Journal*, vol. 41, no. 4, (1998), 1089-1120.

17 *Irish Press*, 13 March 1950.

18 *Sunday Independent*, 19 March 1950.

19 Robin Roe, interview, 21 April 2004.

20 *Connacht Sentinel*, 27 Jan. 1953.

21 The Irish team, with place of birth and club was as follows:
Robin Gregg: Ballymena (Queen's University Belfast); Maurice
Mortell: Cork (Bective Rangers); Noel Henderson: Derry (NIFC);
Robin Godfrey: Dublin (UCD); Joey Gaston: Ballymena (Dublin
University); Seamus Kelly: Wexford (Lansdowne); John O'Meara:
Cork (UCC); Gordon Wood: Limerick (Garryowen); Robin Roe:
Ballybrophy (Dublin University/Lansdowne); Fuzzy Anderson:
Belfast (Queen's University Belfast); Paddy Lawlor: Dublin
(Clontarf); Robin Thompson: Belfast (Instonians); Jim McCarthy:
Cork (Dolphin); Ronnie Kavanagh: Dublin (Wanderers); Gerald
Reidy: Cork (Dolphin).

22 James McCarthy, interviews, 27-28 April 2004.

23 Roe, interview, 21 April 2004.

24 Letter from Maurice Mortell to Vic Rigby, 22 April 2004.

25 Ibid.

26 Ibid.

27 Roe, interview, 21 April 2004.

28 McCarthy, interviews, 27-28 April 2004. McCarthy was mistaken
in his assertion that Hanrahan was president that season. The
position was, in fact, held by J.B. O'Callaghan, an Ulsterman, but
he would not have been at this informal meeting because he was
not a southerner.

29 *Irish Times*, 23 Nov. 1989.

30 Letter from Mortell to Rigby, 22 April 2004.

31 McCarthy, interviews, 27-28 April 2004.

32 Email from Fuzzy Anderson to Vic Rigby, 30 March 2004.

33 There has been some suggestion that Irish lock Paddy Lawlor
deliberately disrespected the British national anthem. One
account has it that: 'He [Lawlor] did not stand at all but shuffled

and walked about, pulled at his pants etc, etc with studied contempt for the duration of the playing of the insulting music. We were thrilled and cheered.' (Letter from Conor O'Kelly to Vic Rigby, 20 May 2004). This suggestion has been dismissed by Jim McCarthy as 'poppycock'. (McCarthy, interview)

34 *Irish Press*, 2 March 1954.

35 McCarthy, interview.

36 Diffley, *Men in Green*, p. 49.

37 Email from Thompson to Rigby, 8 March 2004.

38 Roe, interview.

39 McCarthy, interview.

40 *Irish Press*, 2 March 1954.

41 Letter from Grant Weatherstone to Victor Rigby, 14 April 2004.

42 Letter from Robert McEwen to Vic Rigby, 8 March 2004.

43 R. MacGinty, 'The political Use of Symbols of Accord and Discord: Northern Ireland and South Africa', *Civil Wars*, vol. 4, no. 1(2001), 1–21.

8 LOCATING THE CENTRE: IRISH TRADITIONAL MUSIC AND RE-TRADITIONALISATION AT THE WILLIE CLANCY SUMMER SCHOOL

1 For a more detailed description of the school see Tony C. Kearns and Barry Taylor, *A Touchstone for the Tradition: The Willie Clancy Summer School* (Dingle, 2003).

2 In the early years of the school, classes were given in uilleann piping, fiddle, flute and tin whistle. This expanded in the 1980s

to include concertina and button accordion. The banjo and harmonica were added in 2005 and the harp in 2007. Set-dancing and old style step-dancing classes are taught and a workshop series in traditional singing takes place.

3   Leith Davis, *Music, Postcolonialism, and Gender: The Construction of Irish National Identity, 1724–1874* (Notre Dame, Ind., 2006).

4   Ciarán Mac Mathúna, *The Pipering of Willie Clancy, Volume 1* (Dublin, 1980).

5   Jackie Small, interview, October 2009.

6   Muiris Ó Rócháin, interview, May 2009.

7   See http://comhaltas.ie/events/competitions/ [accessed 31 Oct. 2012].

8   For further information on this see Rachel C. Fleming, 'Resisting Cultural Standardisation: Comhaltas Ceoltóirí Éireann and the Revitalisation of Traditional Music in Ireland', *Journal of Folklore Research,* 41 (2004), 227–57; and Méabh Ní Fhuartháin, 'Comhaltas Ceoltóirí Éireann: Shaping Tradition, 1951–1970' (PhD Thesis, NUI Galway, 2011), pp. 281–333.

9   Séamus Mac Mathúna, 'Today and Tomorrow: A Critical Appraisal of the State of Traditional Music', *Fonn,* 2 (1964), 61–63.

10 Eamon Ó Muirí, 'The Fleadh', *Fonn* 2 (1964), 67–69.

11 Ó Rócháin, 2009.

12 This in no way disregards the role of Comhaltas in celebrating older tradition-bearers, but is a general comment on the challenges presented, particularly during the 1960s, to the identity of the Fleadh.

13 For further details about this see Kearns and Taylor, *A Touchstone for the Tradition: The Willie Clancy Summer School* (Dingle, 2003), pp. 64–65.

14 Mac Mathúna, 'Today and Tomorrow: A Critical Appraisal of the state of Traditional Music', 61–63.

15 A positive outcome for both organisations resulted, with the first Willie Clancy Week providing the model for subsequent highly successful Scoil Éigse discussed in detail later in the essay.

16 See Barbara O' Connor, '"Come and daunce with me in Irlande": Tourism, Dance and Globalisation', in Michael Cronin and Barbara O'Connor (eds), *Irish Tourism: Image, Culture, and Identity* (Clevedon; Buffalo, 2003); Martin McLoone, *Film, Media and Popular Culture in Ireland: Cityscapes, Landscapes, Soundscapes* (Dublin, 2008); and Noel Mclaughlin and Martin McLoone, 'Hybridity and National Musics: The Case of Irish Rock Music', *Popular Music,* 19 (2000), 181.

17 Diarmuid Ó Giolláin, 'The National and the Local: Practices of De- and retraditionalisation', *FF Network,* 28 (2005), 10–18.

18 Following Bourdieu, the term 'cultural capital' is used throughout this essay to express the social value of the skills and dispositions embedded in cultural competence and experience. Pierre Bourdieu, 'The Forms of Capital', in J.G. Richardson (ed.), *Handbook of Theory and Research for the Sociology of Education* (New York, 1986), pp. 241–258.

19 Vincent Griffin from east Clare has also taught at the school since its inception.

20 Contemporary teaching methods at the school would frequently involve breaking a tune down into smaller phrases. After sustained repetition and acquisition of a phrase, the tutor would move onto the next one and eventually piece these phrases together into an entire tune. Máire O'Keefe (in an interview in December 2009) described how the older musicians approached teaching in a manner closer to performance, 'playing away' a

given tune in its entirety and continuously repeating it until students managed to pick it up and join in.

21 Denis Liddy, interview, July 2010.

22 Pierre Bourdieu, *Outline of a Theory of Practice* (Cambridge, 2007), p. 21.

23 This took place during the Willie Clancy Summer School 2009.

24 James Kelly's class at the Willie Clancy Summer School 2009.

25 Both Vincent Griffin and Sean Keane attended the early summer schools. Griffin is a fiddle player from Feakle in east Clare. Sean Keane was a member of Ceoltóirí Chualann and still plays with the Chieftains.

26 Brendan Mulvihill, son of Martin Mulvihill, a fiddle player from Glin, Co. Limerick.

27 John McFadden, a fiddle player from Co. Mayo was recorded by music collector Captain Francis O'Neill in Chicago in 1907. Further information on the O'Neill cylinders is available here: http://archives.irishfest.com/dunn-family-collection/History/ONeill-Cylinders.htm [accessed 1 Nov. 2012].

28 Joe Cleary, 'Preface', in J. Cleary and C. Connolly (eds), *The Cambridge Companion to Modern Irish Culture* (Cambridge, 2004), xiii.

29 Joe Cleary, 'Introduction: Ireland and Modernity ', in Joe Cleary and Claire Connolly (eds), *The Cambridge Companion to Modern Irish Culture* (Cambridge, 2004), p. 5.

30 Philip V. Bohlman, 'Irish Music at the Edge of History', in Thérèse Smith (ed.), *Ancestral Imprints: Histories of Irish Traditional Music and Dance* (Cork University Press, 2012), pp. 181–206.

31 Indeed, this would add to what Arjun Appadurai would describe as its de-territorialisation as well. See Appandurai, *Modernity at*

Large: Cultural Dimensions of Globalization (Minneapolis and London, 1996), pp. 27–47.

32 Séamus Ennis collected in County Clare in 1945 for the Irish Folklore Commission and in 1949 for RÉ. Ciarán Mac Mathúna began his collecting in Clare in 1955 for RTÉ radio and later television. Tom Munnelly began collecting in County Clare from 1971 and relocated there in 1978. The subsequent broadcasting of collected materials contributed to the legacy of County Clare as a site for Irish traditional music.

33 Bohlman, 'Irish Music at the Edge of History', p. 189.

34 Examples include the South Sligo Summer School in Tubbercurry, Co. Sligo and the Joe Mooney Summer School in Drumbshanbo, Co. Leitrim.

35 John O' Flynn, *The Irishness of Irish Music* (Aldershot, 2009), p. 11.

9 LIFE ON-AIR: TALK RADIO AND POPULAR CULTURE IN IRELAND

1 *Irish Times*, 29 Nov. 1995.

2 Kathleen Hall Jamieson, *Call-in Political Talk Radio: Background, Content, Audiences, Portrayal in Mainstream Media* (Annenburg, 1986).

3 Andrew Crisell, *Understanding Radio* (London, 1986), p. 384.

4 Ibid.

5 Ibid.

6 *Sunday Independent*, 14 Dec. 1980.

7 *Irish Times*, 18 Dec. 1993.

8 Ibid.

9 *Irish Independent,* 19 Nov. 1980.

10 *Irish Times,* 18 Dec. 1993.

11 Myra MacDonald, *Representing Women: Myths of Femininity in the Popular Media* (London, 2009), p. 45.

12 Ibid.

13 *Irish Examiner,* 11 Sep. 2008.

14 'Broadcasting Authority of Ireland: Public Consultation on the Draft Code on Fairness, Impartiality and Accountability in News and Current Affairs', 2012.

15 Ibid.

16 *Harvard International Journal of Press/Politics* (London, 1991), pp. 57–79.

17 *Irish Times,* 3 Nov. 1989.

18 Ibid.

19 *Inside Radio,* (3 Vols. 2003), p. 7.

20 *Irish Times,* 14 Oct. 1989.

21 Ibid.

22 Warren K. Agee, *Introduction to Mass Communications* (12th edition, London, 1997), p. 277.

23 www.rte/2fm/ryanshow. [accessed: 5 May 2009].)

24 *Irish Times,* Michael Foley, 15 Sep. 1988.

25 The name comes from *Morning Zoo.* This is the format of morning radio shows common in English-language radio broadcasting. The name is derived from the 'wackiness and zaniness' of the activities and overall personalities of the show and its hosts.

26 Ibid.

27 *Irish Times,* 17 Apr. 1990.

28 Bibi Baskin is a former RTÉ presenter who hosted her own Saturday night talk show on RTÉ television.

29 *Sunday Independent,* Niamh Horan, 9 May 2010.

30 *Irish Times,* 27 Oct. 1990.

31 *Irish Examiner,* 7 May 2010.

32 *Sunday Independent,* 12 Dec. 1999.

33 *Sunday Independent,* 21 Sep. 2008.

34 Ibid.

35 *Irish Examiner,* 17 Sep. 2009.

36 www.96fm.ie [accessed 18 June 2012].

37 www.radiokerry.ie/presenters.

38 RTÉ Radio JNLR's, 17 Nov. 2011.

39 *Sunday Independent,* 13 Sep. 2009.

40 Ibid.

41 Ibid.

42 Bertolt Brecht, 'The Radio as an Apparatus of Communication', in J. Willett (ed.), *Brecht on Theatre: The Development of an Aesthetic* (London, 1964), p. 61.

43 *Irish Times,* 29 Nov. 1995.

44 Ibid.

45 *Sunday Independent,* 6 Apr. 1997.

46 Paddy Scannell, *Broadcast Talk* (London, 1991), p. 3.

47 Ibid.

48 Ibid.

49 Ibid.

50 *Irish Examiner*, 13 Mar. 2011.

51 JNLR, 2010–2011.

52 *Irish Examiner*, 13 Mar. 2011.

10 NEITHER WHITE NOR FREE: IRISH RAILROAD WORKERS IN THE TROUBLED COLONY OF CUBA, 1835–1837

1   Brian K. Axel, *From the Margins: Historical Anthropology and its Futures* (Durham, 2002), p. 15.

2   David Turnbull, *Travels in the West: Cuba with Notices of Porto Rico and the Slave Trade* (London 1840), Replica edition by Elibron Classics (New York, 2005), p. 190.

3   Manuel Moreno-Fraginals, *The Sugar Mill: The Socioeconomic Complex of Sugar in Cuba.* Translated by Cedric Belfrage (New York, 1976), p. 135; Oscar Zanetti and Alejandro García, *Sugar and Railroads: A Cuban History 1837–1959.* Translated by Franklin Knight and Mary Todd (Chapel Hill, 1987), p. 117.

4   Ann Laura Stoler 'Tense and Tender Ties: The Politics of Comparison in North American History and (post) Colonial Studies', *The Journal of American History,* vol. 88, no. 3 (2001), 861.

5   Alexander Von Humboldt, *Political Essay on the Island of Cuba: A Critical Edition,* edited by Vera M. Kutsinski and Ottmar Ette (Chicago, 2011), p. 68.

6   Ada Ferrer, *Insurgent Cuba: Race, Nation, and Revolution, 1868-1898* (Chapel Hill, 1999), pp. 5–7.

7   Turnbull, *Travels in the West*, p. 179.

8   Robert Paquette, *Sugar is Made with Blood: The Conspiracy of Escalera and the Conflict Between Empires over Slavery in Cuba* (Middletown CT, 1988), p. 112.

9   Gema A. Guevara, 'Inexacting Whiteness: *Blanqueamiento* as a Gender-Specific Trope in the Nineteenth Century', *Cuban Studies*, vol. 36, no. 36 (2005), 106.

10 Cited in Duvon Corbitt, 'Immigration in Cuba', *The Hispanic American Historical Review*, vol. 22, no. 2 (1942), 300.

11 Cited in Olga Portuondo Zúñiga, *José Antonio Saco: Eternamente Polémico* (Santiago de Cuba, 2005), p. 155.

12 Guevara, 'Inexacting Whiteness', p. 106.

13 *Mestisaje*, conceived as a dangerous source of subversion, 'it was seen as a threat to white prestige, an embodiment of European degeneration and moral decay'. See Ann Stoler, 'Sexual Affronts and Racial Frontiers: European Identities and the Cultural Politics of Exclusion in Colonial Southeast Asia' in Frederick Cooper and Laura Ann Stoler (eds), *Tensions of Empire: Colonial Cultures in a Bourgeois World* (Berkeley, 1997), p. 199.

14 Guevara, 'Inexacting Whiteness', 107.

15 Verena Martinez-Alier, *Marriage, Class and Colour in Nineteenth-Century Cuba: A Study of Racial Attitudes and Sexual Values in a Slave Society* (Cambridge, 1974).

16 Cited in Corbitt, 'Immigration', p. 295.

17 Oscar Zanetti and Alejandro García, *Sugar and Railroads* (Chapel Hill, 1987), p. 118.

18 Alfred Kruger to the *Comisión de Camino de Hierro*, 1 Aug., 1835, in Archivo Nacional Cubano (ANC) Junta de Fomento (JF), ANC JF, 130-6375.

19 Railroad Commission to Kruger and Wright, Aug. 1835, ANC JF 130–6375.

20 Augustin Ferrety to Tomas Romay, 27 March 1828, ANC JF, 185–8341.

21 Cited in Mathew Mason, '"The Hands Here Are Disposed to Be Turbulent": Unrest Among the Irish Trackmen of the Baltimore and Ohio Railroad, 1829–1851', *Labor History,* vol. 39 (1998), 255.

22 *Diario de La Habana,* 10 Nov. 1835; *Diario de La Habana,* 16 Dec. 1835, (Biblioteca Nacional José Martí, La Habana Cuba, Sala Cubana). For copies of ships' manifests for these four ships see ANC JF, 179-8234.

23 Letter from the American Consul, Nicholas Trist to *Junta de Fomento,* 17 May 1836, ANC JF, 130–6378.

24 Alfonso Ballol, *El camino de Herro de la Habana a Güines: Primer Ferrocarril de Iberoamérica* (Madrid, 1987), p. 94.

25 The peso was on a par with the United States dollar at the time. See Franklin Knight, *Slave Society in Cuba During the Nineteenth Century* (Madison, 1970), p. 30.

26 See ANC JF, 13-6378 for a copy of contract.

27 Ibid.

28 Hugh Thomas, *Cuba: The Pursuit of Freedom* (London, 2001), p. 113 and Richard Gott, *Cuba: A New History* (London, 2005), p. 113.

29 Manuel Fariña-González, 'Las Contratas Isleñas del Ferrocarril La Habana-Güines (Cuba)', in *XIII Coloquio de Historia Canario-Americana 1998* (Las Palmas, 2000), pp. 2102–2109.

30 Kruger to the Railroad Commission, 1 September 1835, ANC JF, 130–6390.

31 Turnbull, *Travels in the West,* p. 190.

32 William W. Watson and J. Francis Watson, *The Ghosts of Duffy's Cut: The Irish Who Died Building America's Most Dangerous Stretch of Railroad* (London, 2006), p. 70.

33 Moreno-Fraginals, *The Sugarmill*, p. 136.

34 The standard Cuban wage was 12 to 25 pesos a month for unskilled labour. Moreno-Fraginals, *The Sugarmill*, p. 135.

35 Thomas C. Holt, Frederick Cooper and Rebecca J. Scott, *Beyond Slavery: Explorations of Race, Labour, and Citizenship in Post Emancipation Societies* (Chapel Hill, 2000), p. 22.

36 Kruger to the Railroad Commission, 1 September 1835, ANC JF, 130–6390.

37 The Railroad Commission to Captain-General, Miguel Tacón, ANC JF, 130–6378.

38 Violeta Serrano, *Crónicas del Primer Ferrocarril de Cuba* (Havana, 1973), p. 38.

39 Ibid., p. 191.

40 Archives, Foreign Office, (hereafter TNA FO), TNA FO, 72/513.

41 *Junta de Fomento* to the Captain-General, 5 July 1836, ANC JF, 130–6378.

42 George Webster to the Captain-General, 17 Feb. 1836, ANC JF, 130–6378.

43 Ibid.

44 Nicholas Trist to Miguel Tacón, 16 May 1836, ANC JF, 130-6378.

45 Nicholas Trist to Miguel Tacón, 24 February 1836, ANC JF, 130-6378.

46 Trist to the *Junta de Fomento*, 16 May 1836, ANC JF, 130-6378.

47 Ann Laura Stoler, 'Developing Historical Negatives: Race and the (Modernist) Visions of a Colonial State', in Axel (ed.), *From the Margins* (Durham, 2002), p. 165.

48 *Junta de Fomento* to the American Consul, 15 March 1836, ANC JF, 130-6378.

49 *Junta de Fomento* to Miguel Tacón, 3 June 1836, ANC JF, 130-6378.

50 *Diario de La Habana*, 4 June 1836.

51 Evelyn Hu-DeHart, 'Opium and Social Control: Chinese Coolies on the Plantations of Peru and Cuba', *Journal of Chinese Overseas*, vol. 1, no. 2 (2005), 171.

52 Ann Laura Stoler, *Along The Archival Grain: Epistemic Anxieties and Colonial Common Sense* (Princeton, 2009), p. 9.

INDEX

Hayden, Tommy 30
Heaney, Seamus 1
Henderson, Noel 110
Hezlet, Major Charles O. (C.O.H.) 54–5
Hiberno-English 68, 187n8
Hogan, Sarsfield 108, 109
Holt, Richard 51
Holt, Thomas 161
Homer 72
Hughes, Joe 102–3, 113
Humboldt, Alexander von 149, 203n5

indentured labourers, in Cuba 146–7, 154, 157, 167
Independent Radio and Television Commission 144
Inglis, Brian 51
IRA, and Rineen ambush 53–4, 185n19
Ireland Act (1949) 112–13
IRFU *see* Irish Rugby Football Union
Irish Book Design Award (1985) 18
Irish Field 51
Irish Folk Song Society 16
Irish Free State 47, 48, 52, 55, 56, 101
Irish Golfer, The 51
Irish Independent 56
Irish Kidney Association 139
Irish Life 51
Irish migrant workers 3, 146–8, 154–6, 162, 165, 167–8
desertion 156, 157, 160, 162, 166
destitution 163–4
perception of 147, 148, 166
wages 165, 167, 205n34
work contracts 156, 157
working conditions 157, 160–1
Irish Music Studies 2
Irish Press 99–100, 102–3, 111, 112
Irish Rugby Football Union (IRFU)
98–9, 193n8, 193n12
British national anthem 99–100
criticism of 104
flag policy 101–2, 113
Irish team (1954) 194n21
and Ravenhill incident 105–11, 113
symbolically neutral flag 101, 113
Irish Studies 4
Irish Times 54, 56, 67, 70, 130, 134–5, 136
Irish Traditional Music Archive 125
Isaacs, Isaac 7

RTÉ 91–2, 129, 131, 144
RTÉ Radio 1 129, 132, 133, 139, 144
RTÉ 2FM 132, 134, 135, 138, 144
rugby
Ireland's Call 99
Irish team (1954) 105, 194n21
origins in Ireland 100–1
and pluralism 98–9
see also Irish Rugby Football Union
Rushe, Desmond 68
Russell, Bertrand 73
Ryan, Gerry 136–7, 138, 142
Ryan, Joe 120
Rynne, Andy 19

Saco, José Antonio 150–1
Satirist 12
Saturday Review 13
Scannell, Paddy 143
Scoil Éigse 126, 197n15
Sexton, Nora 53
sexual puritanism 64–5
Shamrock, The (1830) 11
Shanahan, Jim 4
Shepherd, Jean 28, 41
showbands 3, 23–4, 32–3, 40
perception of women 26–7, 37–8
and women as instrumentalists 28, 44
see also women as showband singers
Simmonds, Gordon 59, 186n36
Sirr, Major 10
Sketches of Ireland Sixty Years Ago 15
slavery 146–7, 149–50
abolition of 150, 152
Smithfield 88–9
Smyth, Brendan 142
Smyth, Gerry 90
songs
and comic operas 8–9
comical 11, 17
and gallows humour 5–6
Irish songs, perception of 11–12
Jemmy O'Brien's Minuet 10, 173n34
political 10
revolutionary 9
satirical 9